A Century of
CHILDHOOD

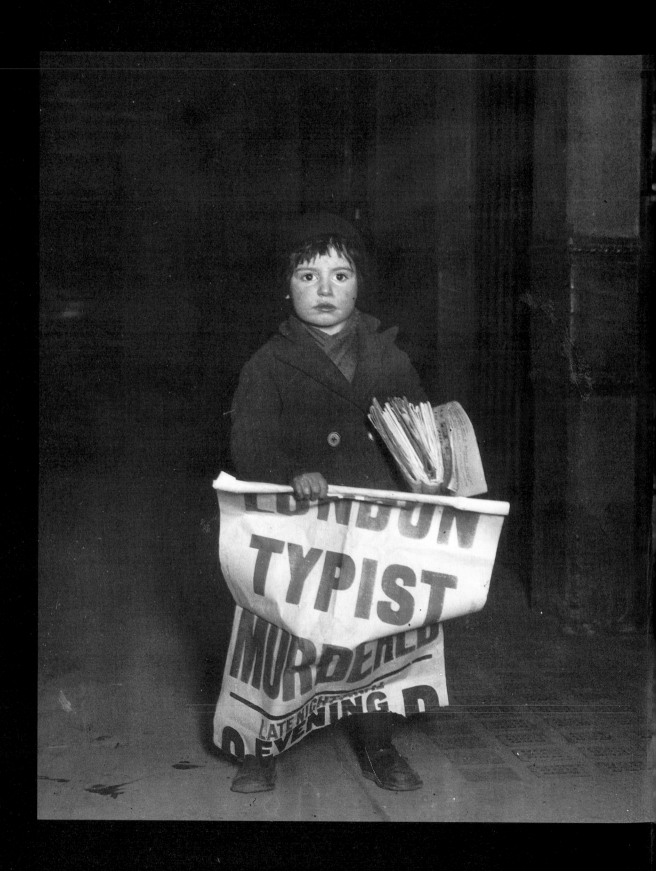

A Century of
CHILDHOOD

Steve Humphries · Joanna Mack · Robert Perks

SIDGWICK & JACKSON
LONDON

in association with
Channel Four Television Company

Half-title illustration: Boy matchseller, 1900
Title page: A five-year-old newspaper seller at her
regular pitch in Covent Garden, London, 1932

First published in Great Britain in November 1988
by Sidgwick & Jackson Limited

First reprint May 1989

Designed by Paul Watkins

Picture research by Robert Perks and Linda Stradling

ISBN 0-283-99755-9 (Hardback)
ISBN 0-283-99756-7 (Paperback)

Photoset by Rowland Phototypesetting Limited
Bury St Edmunds, Suffolk

Printed in Great Britain by
Butler and Tanner Limited,
Frome, Somerset
for Sidgwick & Jackson Limited
1 Tavistock Chambers, Bloomsbury Way
London WC1A 2SG

Contents

Acknowledgements

We would like to thank all those who have in one way or another helped us in writing this book. Special thanks to Colin Ward for a detailed reading of the final draft and for his perceptive comments. Also to Naomi Sargant of Channel Four for advice on the conceptual shape of the television series which this book accompanies. Linda Stradling, Maggi Cook, Em Kirkpatrick, Mary Pyke, Nikki Clemens, Mike Fox, Fraser Barber and Paola Ribeiro Boulting have helped overcome the many problems we have encountered during the project, as well as making their own special contributions towards both the book and the series. At Channel Four, Godfrey Thorpe has given us much assistance with the organization of the project.

We are also indebted to Paul Thompson, Elizabeth Roberts from the Centre for North West Regional Studies, Lancaster University, Penny Summerfield, Bill Williams and Ros Livshin, Anna Davin, Jonathan Gathorne-Hardy, Colin Holmes of Sheffield University, Diana Dick, Trish Adams, Rob Wilkinson, Faith Eaton, Christina Hardyment, Tony Jowitt of Leeds University, David James of Bradford District Archives, Carol Greenwood of Bradford Central Library, Tim Smith, Olive Howarth and Jan Godbold of Bradford Heritage Recording Unit, Siobhan Kirrane of the Leicester Oral History Project, Donny Hyslop of Southampton Museum's Oral History Section, Ambleside Oral History Project, Kingston Oral History Project, Isobel Mitchell of the Shetland Oral History Project, Helga Hughes of Kirklees Sound Archive, Ken Howarth of the North West Sound Archive, Gill Freeman of Ripon Oral History Project, Mantle Oral History Project, West Newcastle Local Studies, Flashback, Liverpool Local Studies Library, the Oral History Society, Gill Greaves of York Castle Museum, Allan Redfern of Crewe and Alsager College, Doc Rowe and Rosemary Dixon of London Sound and Video Archive, Ian Raison of Rowntree's, York, May Blair, Jonathon Bell, Jim Bradley, Philomena Oakley, Sandy Row, Hammer, Ardoyne and Divis Day Centres in Belfast, Freda Millett and Debra Walker of Oldham Local Interest Centre, Joyce Hammond of Walsall Local History Centre, Gareth Griffiths, Market Harborough Museum, Bradford Museum Service, Nora Marshall of Bethnal Green Museum of Childhood, Marguerite Fawdry of Pollock's Toy Museum, Edinburgh Museum of Childhood, National Children's Bureau, Martin Rosenbaum of the Children's Legal Centre, Debbie Derrick of the National Council for One Parent Families, the Scout Association, Veronica Hird of the Girl Guides' Association, Arthur Flitter of

Haggas's textile mill, near Keighley, Yorkshire, in 1908. In the 1900s over 150,000 children aged twelve and thirteen worked half-time in textile mills in the industrial North

Overleaf: Lord Bath as a boy (seated at the front) with his family at Longleat House during a visit by the future King George V and Queen Mary, June 1909

the Stedfast Association of the Boys' Brigade, Doug Bourn of the Woodcraft Folk, George Rushton of the Band of Hope Union, NSPCC, RNIB, Child Poverty Action Group, Highgate Institute, Parent-Link, Kentish Town, Marion Hood of the Corstorphine Youth Centre, Edinburgh, Zoë Redhead of Summerhill School, Leiston, Suffolk, Christchurch Primary School, Camden, the Cotswold Centre, Ashton Keynes, Aileen Scoular of Welbeck P.R., and Carey Smith of Sidgwick and Jackson. Thanks also to the hundreds of local newspapers and local radio stations that ran appeals and features for us during our research; and to those local history libraries and archives around the country, many of them under-staffed and under threat, which helped us along the way.

Finally, thanks to Sally Humphries, Harold Frayman and Jane Tyrtania who have given us much help and support throughout. And thanks to Emma and Katherine Fatherley, and Helen and Peter Pughe-Morgan of the 'answer-back generation' for help in shaping our ideas. And, last but not least, thanks to those 1500 or so people who took the time to write to us and tell us about their early lives: many of them appear in this book and we could not have written it without them.

Introduction

CHILDHOOD, as we know it in Britain today, is surprisingly new. The childhood world inhabited by boys and girls of the late 1980s is almost unrecognizable compared to that in which their grandparents and great-grandparents grew up. Many children today find it difficult to conceive of a life without leisure parks, video games, school trips, junior discos and a room of their own. Their great-grandparents, however, often remember a very different childhood which was shorter and more brutal, and which revolved around hard labour. These children, brought up before the First World War, found their childhood ended abruptly on their twelfth birthday, when many could legally begin work. It was a time – at least for the children of the working classes – not for parties and presents, but for facing up to adult responsibilities. Parents needed their children's earnings to help in the family's battle for survival, and sons and daughters saw it as their duty to earn a weekly wage as soon as they could.

In this book we chronicle the extraordinary change in the way we treat children from the 'seen-and-not-heard' days of the Edwardian era to the post-Spock liberalism of the 1960s and beyond. We provide the first ever social history of childhood in Britain in the twentieth century. Perhaps one reason why nobody has hitherto tried to document the recent history of this stage of life, is because so much of the child's world is highly subjective and personal. When most of us look back on our young days we remember relationships with our mother and father, our best friends, imaginary games and secret hopes and fears: all these things were central to our childhood. Yet – apart from in a few autobiographies – these experiences are simply not recorded and remain hidden from history. The only way to reach these memories, and thereby to get to the heart of the experience of childhood, is through personal reminiscence. In writing this book (and making the television series which it accompanies) we have collected and considered the childhood stories of more than 1500 people born from the early 1890s up to the 1980s. By drawing on this material we try to provide a unique child's eye view of the experience of childhood. We hear the authentic voice of children who grew up in exclusive boarding schools, in city slums, in suburban homes and in orphanages and reformatories.

We see that it is really only in our century that childhood has been created as a lengthy and protected stage of life. We conclude that it is the twentieth century that truly is *the* age of the child.

THE AGE OF THE CHILD

WE OFTEN associate child labour with the dark satanic mills of Victorian Britain and assume that the great reforms of the nineteenth century eliminated this social evil of the new industrial age. The Victorians did indeed remove many young boys and girls into the relatively protected setting of the schoolroom. However, many were still beginning work at the tender age of twelve or thirteen right up until the early 1920s. This first chapter tells the story of the fundamental change in the work expected of children in the twentieth century, from waged labour to study at school.

During the early part of our century there was a fairly rigid division between boys' and girls' work. Boys were recruited in large numbers for factory work and for the traditional heavy industries, like engineering, shipbuilding and mining. There were a few apprenticeships, but for the most part the work was semi-skilled or unskilled. There were also a host of 'blind alley' jobs as errand boys, messengers, packers and the like, which often ended in unemployment at the age of sixteen or eighteen, when employers turned to a new set of young school leavers who could be paid more cheaply and controlled more easily. One of the most arduous and dangerous jobs undertaken by boys was that of coal-mining. Pit accidents, leading to death or disability among boy miners, continued well into our century. Andrew Harle, born in 1924 in the mining village of Byers Green in County Durham, first went down the pit when he was fourteen – but his life as a miner was cut short by a tragic accident:

The stones just fell and they hit the back of the tub and it landed on me. I was trapped from the waist down, and my leg was twisted round. Two deputies came and dug underneath me leg, and I said 'Cut it off', because you could see it was nearly off. I wanted us to get out rather than be caught again with another fall. But they kept on digging, then they pulled me belt off and strapped my legs together and put us on the stretcher. And they tried to put me in the cage but they couldn't get us in, so they shoved us three mile up the other end of the pit to get me out. The doctor was waiting for us and he took me clogs off, put us in an ambulance and I went to Durham hospital. I lost consciousness then and the next time I come round I was on the operating table and the doctor says, 'I'm sorry son, there's a clot in the main artery; I'll have to take your leg off.' He says, 'Your mother and father isn't here yet.' And I just says to him, 'Do what you think best, doctor.' And he gave me the chloroform and I was out. I was downhearted when I was left with one leg; I thought that's the end of our life.

Previous pages: A family shares a meagre meal in the London slums around the turn of the century

Right: A pit boy operates
the rope haulage system
for coal tubs at Ashington
colliery in Northumber-
land in 1924. At the same
pit in 1911 (below) a pit
boy and his pony take a
train full of coal tubs
back to the pit-head

The main jobs for girls were to be found in domestic service, dressmaking, and in shops, offices and factories. Domestic service was far and away the most important occupation for women, with 1.5 million 'in service' just before the First World War, many of them girls in their teens. At this time around one in four of all teenage girls were in residential domestic service. The domestic's life involved long hours, low wages and subservient behaviour to the master and mistress. Occasionally it was all too much to bear for girls of an independent spirit. Louise Ross was a parlour maid in Bath just after the First World War:

Left: Scrubbing steps in Manchester before the First World War. Household chores prepared working-class children for a life of manual labour

Above: Children help out with haymaking in Cumbria around the time of the First World War. Many would play truant from school in order to help their parents at harvest-time

I didn't want to go into service but girls didn't have much choice in those days – you had to take what you could get. The first job I did, I was only thirteen, was in a big house. Very opulent it was. I had to be up at six and it was non-stop work all day until bedtime at ten at night. It was humiliating, because you had to do all the most menial things with very little thanks. And the living conditions were terrible. I was cooped up in a tiny attic at the top of the house with hardly room to move. Well, one day I just couldn't stand it any longer. I was told to clean the master's boots, they were filthy, and I thought, 'Why can't he do them himself? Other people have to!' So I refused and I ran away home, never went back again. My step-father went up and collected my little tin trunk with my things in. But I had to get another job in service because that's all there was for a girl with no education.

In rural areas many boys and girls had traditionally been employed at hiring or mop fairs. Most of these were held annually, and prospective domestic and farm labourers would stand in the market place to be inspected and questioned by local farmers. If they were found suitable a year's contract would be agreed on the shake of a hand. Although this age-old custom was in rapid decline in much of England by the turn of the century, in certain areas it remained an important ritual right into the 1930s. In Northern Ireland most villages continued to have a hiring fair and there were quarterly fairs in the large towns. Would-be workers carried a bundle of clothing with them which showed they were available for hire. Ten pounds a year was the going rate in the inter-war years, and many girls and boys walked for anything up to two days to get from home to the fairs. Rose McCullach was hired in 1922 at the age of thirteen at Strabane hiring fair:

We didn't go to bed the night before we were to be hired. My mother got my clothes together. I didn't have much – just the red petticoat we wore and a vest or two made from bleached flour bags. There would be a lot of us going together, maybe thirty or so children from roundabout – children as young as eleven. We met up on the road about two in the morning and we all walked together in our bare feet. The boys whistled and sang while we went, not realizing what was in front of them. We walked for six hours till we got to the little station and then stopped to put on our boots (they were big heavy boots with iron soles). We got on the train and there were lots of farmers there at the other end to look us over, and we were walked up to where the big clock was in the centre of the fair. The farmers would come up and say, 'Are they fit and strong?' to your mother and 'What do you want for her?' and they'd haggle over the price. Then the farmer took your bundle of clothes to show you were hired and the deal would be clinched with a big bun and a mug of cocoa. And you wouldn't see mother again for six months.

Most boys and girls were able to accept this harsh, early entry into full-time labour because they had worked for their parents from a very young age, helping with domestic chores, child-minding and running errands. In large working-class families the eldest daughter, from the age of seven or eight, often acted as 'little mother' and nursemaid to younger brothers and sisters. She would most likely be responsible for helping to dress and feed them, and for keeping them out of mischief. This would be on top of other chores, like shopping for the whole family. Frances Sherlock, eldest daughter of a family of twelve brought up in Chester in the 1920s, remembers how important her work was to the family's survival:

Certificate of School Attendance for the purpose of employment under Section 5, Elementary Education Act, 1876, or for total or partial exemption under the Bye-Laws.

Ryan Street Council School.

I hereby certify that the following particulars with respect to the Attendances made by the Child named below, at this School after attaining the age of 5 years, are correctly taken from the Registers of the School.

Name in full, and Residence of Child.	Number of Attendances made within the 12 months ending the 31st December.	
Ethel Louisa Cox 67 Ripley St Bfd	1911	380
	1910	380
	1909	374
	1908	386
	1906	325

Signed this ___2___ day of ___Nov___ 1912

Principal Teacher of the above-named School.

* Enter name in full, and state whether a Public Elementary, or Certified Efficient, School.

THIS FORM DOES NOT QUALIFY FOR EMPLOYMENT.

Printed for H.M. Stationery Office by Waterlow Bros. & Layton, Ltd., 24 & 25 Birchin La

Left: A 'half-time certificate', so-called as it exempted twelve-year-olds from school, allowing them to work for wages for five half days a week

Right: A 'little mother' in South Yorkshire between the wars. The eldest daughter would be expected to look after younger brothers and sisters, as well as doing many of the domestic chores

Every other year as I grew up my mother had a baby, which meant that being the eldest I had lots of chores to do and four kids to look after. I had napkins to wash, messages to run. I had to find anything I could to keep the fire going – old shoes, anything that would burn. I'd go along the railway track looking for coal that had dropped off the wagons: more often than not we'd help it off. And I don't ever remember having a chair: mother and father had a chair but we just stood around the table. Everything was hard work then.

When a little older, most children would be employed in a host of part-time jobs before and after school and at weekends, handing over the money earned to their parents. They worked in a wide range of casual occupations, as newspaper sellers, milk boys, street hawkers, errand runners, matchbox makers, child-minders and the like. An investigation into child labour in London in the 1900s found that around a quarter of all schoolchildren, aged between five and thirteen, had paid jobs outside school hours. Probably about half of all schoolboys and schoolgirls aged ten and over were thus in part-time work. Around half worked as errand boys and girls, and another quarter did domestic work or street hawking. A smaller number were involved in light domestic trades, like making matchboxes or artificial flowers. Pay was typically very low, usually less than two shillings (ten pence) for a thirty-hour week. But the moral outcry about child labour in the early years of the century had little effect in reducing the numbers of young children employed. For many families the small extra wages were crucial to their survival. Ted Harrison was born in 1902 in Hoxton, North London, the son of a road-sweeper and the youngest of four children:

16

Opposite, top: A boy helps his parents chop firewood to sell in Manchester around 1900. Inset: A young girl newspaper seller as she was found by Dr Barnardo's around the turn of the century. Bottom: A boy cobbler in the 1930s and (below) working on a milk round in Salford before the First World War

When I was about eight we made artificial flowers at home. I used to be sent to a man called Tommy Green who had sheets of dyed cloth which he punched by hand to make these different shapes of flowers. I had to take them home to me mother with some green paper and wire for the stalks. Then we made all these flowers up and we'd maybe get tuppence a gross or something like that. There would be mother, me brother and me, and me mother used to tell us gory stories about murders or sing us songs to keep us interested. Mind you – we had to bleeding work! We had oil lamps and beer bottles filled with water which we put in front of the lamps to throw the light. We'd work till nine at night but my mother'd work till twelve, especially if she needed the money. When I was nine I got a job with a milkman: oh, that was bloody hard work! I had to get up at five-thirty in the morning, seven days a week, and help him with his cart for three hours before I went to school. It was hard work, especially when the snow was on the ground. He bleeding took advantage of me. He'd be eating bloaters in the coffee shop while I did half his round for him. All for sixpence a week, and me mother had all of it anyway!

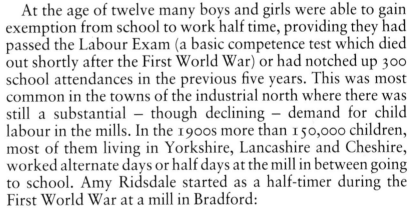

Opposite, above: A family making streamers and (below) wire brushes at home in the East End of London in the 1900s. These were typical of the arduous, low-paid forms of homework which children and parents in poor families had to do to make ends meet

Right: Young winders aged fourteen at Salt's textile mill, Saltaire, West Yorkshire, 1930. Although wages were low – around ten shillings (50p) for a 55-hour week – parents wanted the children to start earning as early as possible

At the age of twelve many boys and girls were able to gain exemption from school to work half time, providing they had passed the Labour Exam (a basic competence test which died out shortly after the First World War) or had notched up 300 school attendances in the previous five years. This was most common in the towns of the industrial north where there was still a substantial – though declining – demand for child labour in the mills. In the 1900s more than 150,000 children, most of them living in Yorkshire, Lancashire and Cheshire, worked alternate days or half days at the mill in between going to school. Amy Ridsdale started as a half-timer during the First World War at a mill in Bradford:

My mother took me that Monday afternoon at quarter past one and handed me over to overlooker and when all machines went on I was petrified, absolutely petrified! I mean, a room with fifty machines in and they all went on – I felt as though I were going to collapse where I were, you see. We started at six o'clock in the morning till half-past eight when we had breakfast till nine. Then nine o'clock till half past twelve, and then we started again at quarter past one until quarter past five. No breaks in between, you know, and I used to have to sit on floor to have me dinner and I used to put me coat down and have forty winks because I was tired. I was a doffer: when spinners had finished we used to have to doff all the full bobbins off you see. It were all right of a job. But I can remember me first week's wage me mother kissing it: I can always remember her kissing it!

An Edwardian child is offered a glass of beer in a public house. Despite the strength of the temperance movement it was legal for children to drink in pubs until 1908

Just as working-class children had to grow up very quickly, so too – but in a different way – did the children of the well-to-do. Many – especially the boys – were sent to preparatory boarding schools at the age of seven or eight. Most 'prepared' their pupils for entry into public school at the age of thirteen. At both it was their duty to learn how to control their emotions, to be 'manly' and to show a stiff upper lip about their early separation from home and parents. The first term could be a traumatic time as boys were removed from cosy and comfortable surroundings into impersonal and institutional regimes where facilities were often of the most spartan kind. Lord Hailsham, born in 1907, was packed off to Sunningdale prep school in 1914:

Of course, I was terribly homesick at first and it was a terrible shock. I was sent there at eight and I'd only learnt how to put on knickerbockers a few days before, and I couldn't tie my tie! We had to get up at seven o'clock in the morning and have cold baths. And, of course, the sanitary arrangements were beyond belief: the earth closets were called 'dubs' and you were assigned to a particular 'dub'. I was assigned to number one and graduated to number twelve by the time I left. You had a ticket and you had to go in a particular order: I can't tell you how disgusting it was! I was flung into this awful dormitory with about thirteen others. One got chilblains in the winter because there was no heating, and the food was disgusting!

In the 1900s the state really conceived and treated children much the same as adults. They were seen as legally responsible for their own behaviour from a very young age. This gave children a degree of independence, and some adult privileges, which today seem quite surprising. For example, at the turn of the century older children enjoyed the right to smoke, drink and gamble. Young children were also often allowed into pubs and there would sometimes be bowls of sweets on the bar to keep them happy while their parents were drinking. Many poorer children would have their first taste of alcohol on those visits to the pub with their parents. Cathy Barnacle, born in London in 1903, remembers drinking in pubs with her mother when she was only six:

Pubs weren't strict at all about children going in. I went with me mum and aunty and I used to have this gin spoon, which was a spoon layered with sugar then topped with gin. I'd have maybe three or four of them in an evening. I thought it was great! I had a real taste for it and I'd go rolling home with mum and aunty half drunk.

However, the treatment of children as 'little adults' meant that they were seen as criminally responsible for their actions and so could be punished and placed in prison much the same as adults. In 1900 there were more than 1500 under sixteen in prison, and double that number were birched each year. Young children could be birched for the most petty offences. Len Napper, born in Bootle on Merseyside in 1907, was only eight years old when he got six strokes of the birch for accidentally setting fire to a tree in his local park:

The police came round to our house and we had to attend court and we were all sentenced to six strokes. When sentence was passed there was complete uproar and bedlam. There were cries of 'This is not British justice!' and the women kicked up hell. It was quite some time before order was restored. We were ushered down to the cells and we could hear a tap running in the next room which was them soaking the birch ready. The next thing was the doctor came to examine us to pass us. After that they came: I being the biggest they took me first. Once you have had the birch you never forget it.

Above and left: Farthing breakfasts at the Salvation Army around 1900. The Salvation Army were in the forefront of the child-saving movement and (right) made a special effort to provide Christmas presents for poor children

Schoolchildren in Blackburn, Lancashire, 1906. The emphasis on regular attendance, enforced by the 'School Board man', removed many children from the world of waged labour

But already by the 1900s a new and more protective approach towards children was increasingly challenging the old view of them as 'little adults'. This approach was enshrined in the 1908 'Children's Charter' which established juvenile courts and treated children as children under the age of fourteen. After this it became illegal to sell tobacco or alcohol to those under fourteen years old. And, more significantly, there was a gradual relaxation in the rules governing the extent to which children of this age could be held to be criminally responsible for their own actions. The practice of sending children to prison alongside adult criminals was finally abandoned, and children who committed crimes were now automatically sent to special institutions, like industrial schools and reformatories. Although these had been established in Victorian times, special institutions for children became more and more important in our century. Their aim was to reform as well as to punish – though, as we see later, the methods they used were sometimes terribly brutal.

The main impact, however, of the challenge to the old view of children as 'little adults' was a growing concern to remove children from the labour market and provide them with compulsory state schooling at an earlier age. This movement had begun during the Victorian period and gained further momentum in the early years of the century with the concern

A class of schoolchildren pictured in Shipley, West Yorkshire, in 1908

about 'boy' and 'girl' labour. The poor quality and physical condition of volunteers for the Boer War also caused great alarm, and many saw the seeds of Britain's imperial ruin in the poor health of young working boys and girls. As a consequence, the school leaving age was extended from twelve to fourteen between 1899 and 1918, and the half-time system ended. Children were now required to do *school* work as opposed to waged labour. But, for the majority, it was school work devised to produce an obedient and unquestioning labour force for the new factories and offices. It often consisted of rote learning of the 'Three R's' (reading, writing and arithmetic) and was of a very harsh nature. Serried ranks of schoolchildren learnt their lessons in an authoritarian atmosphere. Punishment was severe and the cane was frequently used for virtually any misdemeanour. Ted Harrison went to Canal Road School in Hoxton, North London, before the First World War:

We were in fear of the teachers: we didn't know where they came from or where they went. They were very strict and you had to salute them. Jones the Welshman was the worst: he was a proper sadist and he'd drag you out by your hair to the front for the slightest thing. He give you a two-hander or a four-hander or a six-hander with the cane. And he held it right over his shoulder and really bring it down hard. Either that or you had to stand in the corner at the front with a dunce's hat on: it was a white conical hat with a black 'D' on. I got punished because I couldn't see the board 'cause I was short-sighted. Every time you were bad you got your name put in red ink in the punishment book, which you had to fetch from the headmaster: it was like carrying the bleeding Cross. They told you that it would be there to carry us all through life. Everything was done sing-song and we never really knew what we were doing.

However, poverty meant that many families still needed their children to go into domestic labour to earn money in order for the whole family to survive. This led to widespread truancy which was as high as 20 per cent in the poorest parts of cities like Glasgow and Liverpool in the early 1900s. Truancy was particularly prevalent among large families in which the father was dead or unemployed, and in country districts where there was a huge demand from farmers for seasonal labour in the fields. Much of the male truancy, especially in rural areas, was concentrated in the summer months when boys were needed for the harvest. Among girls, truancy was highest on washdays (Mondays) and on Fridays (which was a big cleaning day), when they would be required to help at home or look after younger brothers and sisters. In

Barge children on the Grand Union Canal in the 1920s. Although it was illegal, many young canal children helped to steer barges, tend horses and open locks: few went to school

some cases, if a girl was absent from school, a blind eye was turned by the attendance officer, or 'Board man' as he was known. Elsie Unwin, brought up in Liverpool in the early years of the century, regularly played truant from school:

I spent a lot of time sagging [Liverpool slang for truanting]. Yes, I'd be sitting there on the doorstep when I should have been at school. Mum wanted me to look after the little ones and I'd push them in the pram or play with them in the street. The old School Board man, he caught me sometimes and he threatened to take me away, but I wasn't worried. I thought my life can't be any harder than it is now. You see, we were very poor; we hardly had enough to eat. But they never did anything.

But improvements in the standard of living and a gradual reduction in the size of families meant there was less demand for child labour at home and slowly attendance at school improved. By the 1920s school attendance rates were over 90 per cent. And in the evenings and at weekends increasing numbers of children were released from some of their old domestic duties and were able to begin to enjoy the benefits of the new protected world of childhood. There was more free time and a little more money to spare, so that working-class children could enjoy cycling or swimming with their friends, or perhaps visit the circus or the zoo with their parents.

By the 1920s and 1930s there were only a few very poor social groups who saw their children principally as sources of labour and who regularly withheld them from school. Most were travelling people, such as canal children who worked the barges with their families and only occasionally attended schools along the way. Jack Meredith was born on a barge in Wolverhampton in 1912, and he spent most of his childhood days helping his mother and father run the horse-drawn canal boats they operated for a Black Country firm:

I reckon I only spent a couple of months at school in all my young days – that's the reason I can't read or write today. What I'd do, I'd go to a school in the morning, sign in, but by eleven o'clock my mother would come and collect me and we'd be off on the barges again. I must have gone to hundreds of schools near the canals, but I was only a few hours in each one, then I might be off on the boat for a few months. I started steering when I was seven, but my real job was looking after the old horse, feeding him and when we went through a tunnel I'd lead him over the top. Then I'd help with the lock gates. You'd always be on the look out for the inspectors because you weren't meant to do anything till you were fourteen but they never caught us.

The new protective attitudes were also affecting middle- and upper-class children. The old approach, whereby emotional control and manliness was cultivated by initiating the child into the 'adult' world at a very young age, was now less fashionable. There was a new interest in learning through play in the younger years leading to a massive growth of 'educational' toys. Meccano sets, invented by Frank Hornby in 1901, came to be seen as an essential toy for developing the imagination and practical skills of boys, and by the 1930s there were few middle-class toycupboards without one. The later years of childhood were increasingly seen as a time for learning and intellectual exploration which began to find expression in a much broader based curriculum in the grammar and public schools. The muscular Christianity and the cult of athleticism of the nineteenth century was beginning to give way to a new educational emphasis on individual development.

The growing protection of children in the world of education and play, and their removal from the world of paid work, helped to stimulate a new popular custom of childhood – pocket money. Children no longer earned money themselves; they were given it by parents. Fathers usually doled it out to sons and daughters on a Friday night or Saturday morning after they had been paid themselves. It became known among millions of children as the 'Friday penny' or the 'Saturday penny'. Children might supplement their pocket money by running errands, but by the inter-war years a penny a week from mum or dad was seen by most children as their right. Increasingly they spent their money on sweets or going to the cinema, both of which were becoming more and more important in the new childhood. Mary Willmott was born in 1917, the youngest of eight children, in Rushden, Northamptonshire:

We weren't paid for doing jobs around the house, and the boys weren't expected to do any chores anyway. But every Saturday I had one penny which I sometimes put in the Co-op Penny Bank. There was always a queue there on Saturday mornings. Sometimes we spent our one penny on a ha'p'orth of stickjaw and perhaps a few aniseed balls or a sherbet dab. And in the winter I had an extra penny to go to the pictures to see Charlie Chaplin or Jackie Coogan or Tom Mix.

A lot of pocket money was also spent on comics. Comics had originally been aimed largely at young working-class adults, but by the 1920s most were geared to the new pocket

A 'cliffhanger' at a children's cinema matinée in 1940. Between the wars going to the cinema became a popular new way of spending Friday and Saturday pennies

money market of older children. One of the most popular comics was *The Magnet* which by the late 1920s had reached a peak circulation of over 200,000 copies a week. Twelve- and thirteen-year-old elementary schoolboys developed a surprising addiction to Frank Richard's Greyfriars School stories, while Billy Bunter became a cult figure in the slums. To poor boys the boarding-school world seemed immensely exciting and boys from Bethnal Green and Salford adopted some of the phrases of their social superiors calling each other 'old chap' and 'you blighter'.

This new world for the child was to continue apace after the war, especially in the affluent years of the 1950s. The growing desire to spend time and money on children was reflected in the post-war boom in the toy industry and the dramatic increase in present-giving on birthdays and at Christmas. Before the war children's birthdays had been little celebrated amongst the working classes. Now, increasingly, there were parties and presents and the birthday started to become a celebration of what it was to be a child.

The great educational reforms of the immediate post-war years also seemed to be a guarantee of an extended and protected childhood for all, free from the pressures of adult work. These reforms raised the school-leaving age to fifteen, created the 11 plus exam and the secondary modern school. For younger children there were many benefits with the increasing emphasis on the importance of play and imaginative activities in junior schools. However, one major effect of the reforms was to widen the scope and importance of the examination system. In some junior schools lessons for older pupils were geared to passing the 11 plus exam, putting pressure on children at a very young age. Many children who failed this exam ended up at secondary modern school, and often felt inferior and resentful about their treatment. Some rejected school work, resisted teachers' efforts to control them and longed for 'adult' waged labour and an 'adult' status. At a time when jobs were in abundance older children were beginning to turn against the concept of 'childhood' foisted on to them.

These disenchanted boys and girls eagerly embraced the new teenage culture which emerged from the 1950s onwards. Teddy Boys, Mods and Rockers (sub-cultures which offered pupils a new identity and exciting new interests), all had their devotees and followers in schools – especially in secondary modern schools. In adopting the rebellious stance of the 'teenager' (a word borrowed from the Americans during the

31

Second World War), pupils added to tensions in the classroom and made others aware of their sense of resentment at still being treated like children.

Rebellious cults, like that of the Teddy Boy, originated among young workers in their mid to late teens who were enjoying the fruits of affluence. According to some estimates by the mid 1960s their earnings were four times greater than they had been thirty years before. Added to this, most working-class families were now so much better off that there was a break-down in the old tradition whereby teenage sons and daughters had handed over most of their wages to their parents in order to help pay family bills. This meant that, for the first time ever, young people were economically independent and had a substantial amount of disposable income. It was estimated in the early 1960s that the average weekly wage of teenagers was around £10; of this, about £7 was left as disposable income after they had paid for their 'keep' at home. They now had the money to dress distinctively, to go to their own clubs and to buy their own records. This new 'youth culture' quickly made an impact all over Britain. Yvonne Wilson was a young teenager in the small market town of Kendal, in the Lake District, in the late 1950s and early 1960s:

My main memory is of coffee bars and being able to go out to the pictures and then to the coffee bar and sit for ages talking to friends. Then going to a local dance on a Saturday night, and, as the evening drew to a close and the live band was playing a Shadows tune, how we would form lines. There'd be row after row of us doing the Shadow walk. The atmosphere was electric!

For schoolboys and schoolgirls the key to joining this new youth culture was money. But despite the fact that pocket money was increasing in real terms year after year – until it reached an average of five shillings (twenty-five pence) a week by the late 1960s for most fourteen year olds – it still wasn't enough to buy what these young people wanted. Between the mid 1950s and the mid 1960s crime doubled among children. Often the objects of crime conferred on them an adult status. For example, joy-riding in cars started to become one of the most common crimes. In Liverpool, Manchester and London children as young as ten or eleven years old were becoming adept at 'taking and driving away' and boasted of brave exploits being chased by the police or having a crash. Mickey Rooney, born in Manchester, was one of the child joy-riders in the city in the late 1950s and early 1960s:

Teddy Boys in a canteen set up in South London by Dulwich College Mission in 1955 'to keep them off the streets'. With their distinctive dress 'Teds' were part of a youth rebellion which grew out of the new affluence of the 1950s

I remember the first car I had, it was a Zephyr. I saw it there at the corner of our street, and somebody had left the windows down. I was only eleven and I was very small for my age but I knew how to drive a car – you see I'd watched my dad do it. So I went in to the house, got some cushions, put them on the seat and I was away. 'Course, I was in first gear all the way – couldn't change the gears. And I had the windows down, shouting out to me mates, 'Look at me! Come on! Get in!' Only went a few streets away then we dumped it, but I felt like somebody. That was the business; I'd seen it on the Elvis films; the big car! It was exciting, and after that I did it again and again.

Many other schoolchildren increasingly took part-time jobs on Saturdays and in the evenings to get the money they wanted. Some even played truant to take day-time jobs. This became increasingly common amongst secondary modern and comprehensive schoolchildren after the raising of the school-leaving age to sixteen in 1973. By January 1975 a survey showed over 200,000 fifteen year olds absent on just one day, and in one London comprehensive only two-thirds of

children were regularly attending. The increase in the school-leaving age had compelled around a quarter of a million children to stay on, and this fuelled resentment among those children who already felt that ten years of schooling was more than enough. Some took their anger out through vandalism in the classroom. Between 1966 and 1976 the cost of such damage in Manchester schools alone spiralled from £22,000 to £186,000.

The new youth culture also had its attractions for many middle-class children who, due to the growing importance of certification, increasingly found themselves still at school up until the age of seventeen and eighteen. They came under pressure to study for longer and longer hours to get good 'O' and 'A' levels, while the temptations of the new independent world of youth seemed greater and greater. Some became interested in the popular fashions of the day, while others became heavily influenced by middle-class youth sub-cultures like the Beatniks and Hippies, which were much more bohemian and individualistic than their working-class counterparts. The styles of dress which they adopted – for boys this often meant long hair – quickly brought them into conflict with parents and teachers.

In battles between individual pupils and teachers the children invariably lost. So, to resist more effectively the unwanted interference of the school authorities in their lives, some children turned to collective action. The inspiration for this action came from the radical student movements of the late 1960s and most of the early initiatives came from middle-class children at places like Manchester Grammar School. But very soon children at all kinds of schools were involved in the new protest movement.

One expression of this new conflict was the formation of the National Union of School Students in May 1972. During the 1970s the union staged a series of school strikes aimed at establishing basic rights and issued a School Students' Charter. This Charter made five demands: no corporal punishment (then still used in most schools), no uniforms, no petty rules, no prefects and no secret files. Scotland and London were the major centres of activity. In 1972 500 girls in a Glasgow school protested against a school rule that they must wear skirts by turning up in trousers. There were numerous other days of action and membership of the NUSS quickly reached 12,000. Partly in response to these protests many schools made concessions to pupil demands and became more relaxed about uniforms and school rules at least with older children.

Supporters of the National Union of School Students burn their school ties during a march in May 1972, in protest against school uniform and corporal punishment

By the 1980s most schools had become more liberal and more respectful of basic pupil rights than they had been twenty years earlier. The NUSS disappeared, partly because the old anger had been dissipated.

However, in recent years a new focus of resentment has helped to revive political activity among schoolchildren. During the mid 1980s there have been some of the largest school strikes ever seen, most of them concentrated in areas of high unemployment like Liverpool. This is a reflection of an increasingly important division in childhood today: that between the children of the underclass and the children of the fairly affluent majority. For the children of the poor and unemployed who live in the city slums, childhood often remains short and brutal. Some of the poorest children on city 'sink' estates become 'street wise' at a very early age. Addiction to hard drugs like heroin and street crime are now beginning to be recognized as problems among younger and younger children. Being found guilty of mugging is not uncommon now among eight and nine year olds in the most deprived areas of large cities, like Brixton and parts of Notting Hill in London. But, for the majority, childhood in the late 1980s is a lengthy period of protection and indulgence. A host of institutions, from playgroups to toy hypermarkets, exist to satisfy the needs and wants of today's child. Most children of the 1980s enjoy rights and privileges which would have been undreamt of at the beginning of the century.

2. MUM AND DAD

IN THE course of our century there has been a major change in the kinds of emotional relationship formed between children and parents. The shift has been from formality, authoritarianism and distance to informality, libertarianism and closeness. The terms used to describe parents neatly capture this transformation. In Edwardian times children referred to their parents as 'mother' and 'father'. This gradually gave way to the more familiar 'ma' and 'pa'. After this came the ubiquitous 'mum' and 'dad', which has been the most common term for parents since the 1930s. And from the 1960s onwards a minority of liberal, usually middle-class, parents have been happy for their children to be on Christian name terms with them. This chapter explores this movement towards more intimate and informal relationships with parents, and looks at the new problems it has brought in its wake.

During the first decades of the century childhood could often be a traumatic time for both children and parents. Bad housing, poverty and lack of healthcare meant that many working-class children were extremely unhealthy and could expect to experience some serious illness in childhood, particularly in the first years. At the turn of the century the worst infant mortality figure ever was recorded: 163 in every 1000 babies were dying before their first birthday – this compares with around 15 per 1000 today. Most worrying to Edwardian social reformers were the marked differences between the classes. Infant mortality was more than twice as high among the working classes as it was among the middle and upper classes. Where population density was high, overcrowding rife and poor sanitary conditions endemic, infant death was a fact of life. In the poorest parts of cities like Liverpool, the death toll among young babies was appallingly high: around one half died before the age of one. Emma Jones, a young mother in Grimsby in the early years of the century, lost one of her babies during childbirth:

I know I was desperate for a baby boy because I'd lost my Jackie. He was our four year old son, and we'd just lost him with dip, diphtheria. I was heart-broken about that, but I'd kept going thinking I'd have another boy and he'd be my new Jackie. Well, I went into labour, and it was a long and difficult labour, but eventually baby came out. It was a boy. But the doctor held him up in front of me and he said, 'He's useless' and threw him down on the bed. He were dead. He'd been strangled coming out. Of course, I was in a terrible state and they wouldn't let me see my dead baby. My brother came round and wrapped him up in paper and put him

39

in a big margarine box. And because we didn't have any money, he took him on the bus to the grave digger in the cemetery and they put him in a common grave. I don't know where he is to this day. It took me a long time to get over that.

Of those that survived babyhood, one in four children did not survive beyond the age of five. Death cast a shadow over many families, for a host of childhood diseases, which today we immunize against, were then killers. Whooping cough accounted for two-fifths of all deaths under five. Diphtheria and scarlet fever claimed many lives and were made more acute by overcrowding and bed-sharing. Measles killed 7000 children a year in the 1900s. And tuberculosis, although on the decline, was very common among children. Doris Bailey remembers her sister's death from meningitis in Bethnal Green, East London, in 1920:

When she was four, she fell sick one day, and that evening dad took her to the doctor. It was a very rare occasion in our home but dad said he was worried and didn't like the look of her. Early next morning we awakened and heard the unbelievable: a man crying – deep shaking sobs that frightened us all. Mum put her head in the room, her white face with its weepy red eyes, a never-to-be-forgotten sight. 'Get up now,' she said quietly. 'Rosie is dead and there's nothing anyone can do.' Dead! It just wasn't possible. Not our baby. Other people's babies died but not ours. The next days were nightmarish. We all went up to Green Street to buy new clothes. Black coats and dresses and little black felt hats like pudding basins. Our new dresses were black and white check and mum bought yards of black velvet for our Sunday dresses. She took us in the front room, where Rosie lay on the big round table, covered with a white blanket. Never had I seen anything as beautiful as that little statue, in its white lace shroud, surrounded by golden curls. The funeral was not like the street funerals I knew. There was no beer, and it didn't turn into a sing song or a pub crawl as so often happened. The death had a profound effect on us all and changed our life in some ways. There was no radio – no gramophone even – in our house, and nothing broke the quiet stillness of the weeks that followed. Dad sat in his seat watching the pigeons and mum sat with folded hands, not even knitting, just doing nothing, a thing I'd never seen before.

For those children who survived these diseases many con-tinued to suffer from severe dental decay, ear and eye infec-tions, rickets, ringworm, headlice, pneumonia, bronchitis and general under-nourishment. Rowntree's 1901 survey in York found that, on average, boys in workers' families were three-and-a-half inches shorter than boys from upper-class families

A working-class family in
North Shields in 1933

and weighed eleven pounds less. A medical officer reported in
1905 that in a survey of 1000 children he had found only two
possessed a tooth-brush. Girls often suffered more than boys:
they were more likely to have bad eyes due to sewing in poor
light, they had bad backs from looking after younger brothers
and sisters, and suffered more headlice through having long
hair.

If physical survival could be difficult and sometimes
traumatic for children, so too was their relationship with their
parents. Overcrowding in working-class families demanded
discipline and a certain degree of order. The stern moralistic
approach of 'spare the rod' remained strong, especially
amongst the working classes in the North. Sometimes a cane,
a belt or a strap would be left hanging up above the fireplace as
a warning against bad behaviour. This 'seen-and-not-heard'
approach was based on the Evangelical idea of original sin and
the need to break the child's will. Obedience was the prime

NATIONAL SOCIETY
FOR THE PREVENTION OF
CRUELTY TO CHILDREN

INCORPORATED BY ROYAL CHARTER.   PATRON - THE QUEEN.

CROYDON AND DISTRICT BRANCH.

NOTICE.

Information of Ill-treatment or Neglect of Children in this District should be sent to the Hon. Secretary,

LOCAL OFFICE,   Mr. J. G. LINCOLN,

6, PARK STREET, CROYDON.

All further Inquiries, Proceedings, and Expenses will be undertaken by the Society.

Names of Informants kept strictly private.

(Except in cases where malice is proved)

CENTRAL OFFICE,
7, Harpur Street, London, W.C.

BENJAMIN WAUGH,
Director and Secretary.

virtue to be encouraged in all children, and questioning superiors, especially parents, for whatever reason, was often punished. Children were taught that next to their duty to God came their duty to parents. Interestingly, more often than not, it was the mother, responsible for day to day discipline, who inflicted the punishments. The punishments were often most severe in large working-class families, where poverty, cramped living conditions and the noise of many children packed together in the same room all encouraged lost tempers and beatings by parents. Sometimes there was a lack of parental affection too. Jimmy Cooper was born in Bradford in 1906:

My mum used to belt me. She kept a strap on the wringing machine but she used to use her fists as often and I used to ride the punches as best I could. She used to clout me regular and she wouldn't let anyone be close to her, would me mother. She never kissed us or cuddled us or called us 'love', never anything of that description, ever.

In a minority of cases this distant and disciplinarian approach led to child abuse. Child beating was routine in some slum streets and there was a fine line between punishment and abuse. With little local authority regulation, organizations like the NSPCC were only just beginning to have an effect. Children most at risk included those with step-parents: Hilda Shaw was born in Halifax in 1909:

I didn't get a lot of love from my mother, mainly because our house was always full of lodgers. And I had a bad stepfather. He would kick me with his clogs and I spent most of my life in the attic. He'd tie me to the bed with mother's clothes line. It would be hours before mother found me: he had gone off to his waiting-on job at the pub. When I was fourteen he fell while drunk and died from it – it was really then that a new life began for me.

In extreme cases of abuse the authorities would take action, but it would rarely lead to court action, and the unfortunate children were frequently returned to their parents to suffer the same fate again. Vera Butterworth was brought up between the wars in Lancashire and spent her early childhood as a vagrant:

I was born at Jericho, which was the workhouse, and I remember we was always hungry. We'd eat anything – half decaying fruit and anything that we could pinch here and there. I even remember when I was five I queued up to have a feed at a woman's breast because it was all there was. Me mum, dad and three of us kids used to spend

43

Left: An Edwardian nanny and her charge in Bradford, West Yorkshire. Better-off children grew very close to their nannies who often acted as mother substitutes

Opposite: Edwardian children in wealthier families often ate their meals with their nursemaid or nanny. Meals were sometimes only taken with parents on Sunday or on big occasions like birthdays

most of the time on the road, sleeping rough in fields and under hedges. Sometimes we'd sleep in doss houses if my parents had tuppence, but then I used to sleep on the stone floor; there was no beds. We used to collect rags on a cart and we were made to sing for ha'pennies. My parents were always drunk and then they'd be sick or they'd hit us. They used to hit us all the time – it was awful! I've still got the scars! I had pneumonia a lot of the time and when I was bad and we were in Jericho they'd see all the bruises I'd got. But they only kept me there till I was healed, then I had to go back with my parents. There was a shopkeeper in Haslingden saw me and took me in for about nine months and looked after me and gave me father some money. It was heaven! I had new clothes and some knickers which I'd never had before! But my parents took me back and they sold all me clothes. It was awful – I was ill and they reckoned that I'd die but I went back with the shopkeeper when I was eight and after that I never went back with my parents again. But I always had this fear that they would come and take me back again. In fact, when I was fourteen I saw them in town – I couldn't run fast enough! I run home and locked the doors, I was that scared!

In wealthier homes – especially aristocratic ones – parents were also quite often distant figures with whom children had little direct contact. This was the classic 'seen-and-not-heard' upbringing. From birth, well-to-do children would be brought up by nannies and sometimes formed close emotional relationships with them as 'substitute mothers'. Parents would rarely be seen for more than an hour each day; often this would take the form of a story-telling ritual after tea, with the

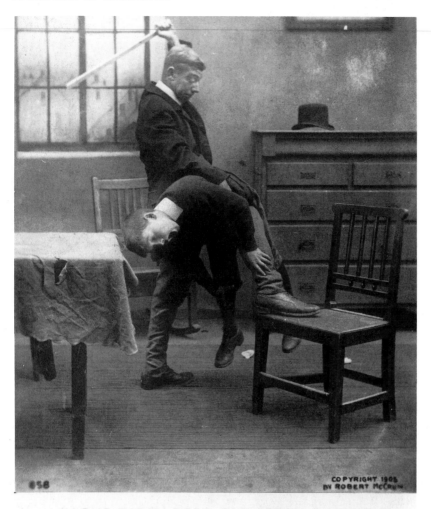

An unusual postcard from
1905 parodies the harsh
Victorian father figure

I LOVE DADDY, DEAR OLD DADDY AND I KNOW
THAT HE LOVES ME.

children being presented for inspection dressed up in their best clothes. Margaret Allen was born in 1892, and her description of distance from her parents, especially her father, typifies upper-middle-class attitudes towards children in the early years of the century:

Father was very strict, and he had his own room which was very much out of bounds to us children. When he was in there we had to be very quiet – there would be trouble if we disturbed him. And we had Fanny who looked after us: in the morning we had breakfast first, then we smartened up and had to sit very still at the table waiting for father. When he came in we had to stand and say, 'Good Morning, Daddy,' and he'd reply, 'Good Morning, children.'

The nursery epitomized the distance between most better-off children and their parents. It was often at the very top of the house, as far as possible from adult life below. Nanny was the absolute ruler and would most likely sleep in a room off the nursery. The nursery was a closed world of toys and make believe where parents rarely ventured, as Lord Hailsham, born in 1907, recalls:

I was much attached to Nurse Field, who was my nanny when I was very young, and she was much attached to me. I was absolutely furious when she went and very deeply upset. I was always aware of my mother but, of course, the nursery was the day-to-day looking after apparatus. The parents went out at night and they came up and said goodnight to you. They were almost divine figures. My mother was more remote than my nanny. Breakfast, lunch and tea would be taken in the nursery and we would eat separately from my parents who would eat in the dining-room. The only exception was on Sundays, when we would come down to Sunday lunch after we'd been cleaned up. I can remember my father being absolutely disgusted with my younger brother dribbling. One or other of my parents would come up and say goodnight, usually not together.

Even older children, out at work, were required to obey their parents absolutely. In particular, the father's word was law, with no room for discussions as to why a particular decision was being made, and certainly not as to whether it was correct. In many working-class families mealtimes had complex sets of rules banning conversation and apportioning what food there was available in a strict pecking order. Father was usually much feared as an authority figure, as May Hackitt, who was brought up in Oldham, Lancashire, around the First World War, recalls:

We had to be seen and not heard, and if they thought that we were listening to their conversation we were told that 'little pigs had big ears'. We had a very strict father and he hit us by a thump on the head if we sniffed up, answered back, didn't walk with our arms swinging and shoulders back, and if we even dared to look at a newspaper, even when we were in our teens. I think my father really hated us; sometimes it seemed he hit us for nothing. He used his leather belt with its brass buckle on us but I think the worst thing was when he kicked us up the backside with his clogs on. They were narrow toed and we called them his arse-kickers.

Parents also had immense influence over their children's choice of friends and courting partners. They tried – often successfully – to control where the couple went, what they did and when they returned home. Girls, in particular, could

expect sanctions and punishments if they were ever late. Lucy
Thirkhill was born in Bradford in 1908:

He was very, very strict was my father: he'd only allow me out on a
Saturday night because he knew that I was near home and knew
everybody who went out more or less. But my dad were so strict. I
had to be home at quarter-past-nine on Saturday night – whatever
happened I'd to be home. And if I didn't get home he used to be sat in
his armchair behind the door, back of the door, and if it were after
quarter-past-nine I'd to run straight upstairs to bed. I couldn't have
any supper, I couldn't have anything. I wasn't often late but when I
were, by jove, I knew about, you know!

Nevertheless, strong bonds of affection were forged in
many families. In working-class families the bonds between
children and parents were often based on shared work and
struggles. Any extra money a child could bring into the family
was more than welcome, and children frequently used to help
with sweated outwork. Grandmothers – and occasionally
grandfathers – also developed close relationships with their
grandchildren, standing in for the mother when she went out
to work. This was common in the Northern textile towns,
where a high proportion of women worked. However, there
were far fewer older people around in the early part of the
century: only 5 per cent of the population were aged over
sixty-five of which half lived with their children. But even if
grandparents were not alive uncles and aunts would be. The
extended working-class family was thus an important survival
mechanism in the early decades of the century. Fred Brewster
was brought up in Islington, North London, just after the
Second World War:

There was my grandma and grandfather always lived at the top, and
on the other three floors there was either my mum and dad and us
kids or, Uncle Jim and Aunt Mink and the kids, Uncle Sid and Aunt
Hat and the kids, and Aunt Polly, the single lady. So we'd be living
in one pair of rooms on the first floor and next minute we'd be down
in the basement. That was all arranged between family. Me grandmother was the real backbone; me grandfather didn't have much to
say. She was the mafia leader, you might say – she pretty well knew
all that was going on. She knew all the medicines that cured things
that didn't cost anything. 'Go up to grandma' and you'd go up and
she'd say, 'Come in, Freddy. What's wrong?' And she'd have the
cure in her chest – all the bits and pieces, you know, herbs and
liquids. And she was a midwife – she used to fetch children into the
world, for the family and for the neighbours if she was needed. She
was well known for it. She'd handle the discipline too, usually
stepping in to stop the kids fighting.

**A Jewish family in
Manchester around 1906**

Even though the harsh and distant 'seen-and-not-heard' relationship with parents was quite common, it was nowhere near as universal as is sometimes supposed. Much more intimate and intense family relationships developed in some ethnic communities, where cultural traditions were quite different. For example, both the Jewish and Italian communities were characterized by particularly intimate and affectionate bonds between parents and their children. And in the Shetlands — where Evangelicalism had little influence — a unique, libertarian approach to child rearing flourished. Here, in the first decades of the century, corporal punishment by parents was practically unheard of — parents controlled their children by reasoning with them. Children were allowed to talk during meals and could leave the table when they wished. They could join in conversation with visitors and took part in their parents' evening activities, often being allowed to stay up late into the night. J. J. Hunter was born in Uyeasound on the small island of Unst in the Shetlands in 1899:

My mother and father were very gentle people and I do remember that they never hit me or used any physical punishment on me in the whole of my young days. And that was true of my brothers and sisters too – mother and father would not hit any of us. Harsh words and a telling off were always enough. You joined in with everything as a child, and most of all that meant helping with all the work that had to be done on the farm, because my father was a small tenant farmer. I'd have to carry the water from the well; I'd help milk the cows; I'd chop firewood; all sorts of things like that from when I was very small. And from the age of six I'd sometimes be up at four in the morning, off cutting peat and bringing it home. It was hard work but it brought us together. The best times, of course, were the dances. I was a fine dancer, and my parents always encouraged me to dance. We were all very happy together.

The traditional strict approach to children remained strong during the first half of the century, but from the 1920s onwards a new, slightly more indulgent and intense, relationship with sons and daughters started to develop. This was the period when the idea of the full-time mother and housewife became immensely popular and powerful. So, too, did the new idea of 'mothercraft' – a science of clear-cut rules, the observance of which was thought to ensure healthy babies. With improvements in the standard of living and reductions in family size, mothers could devote more and more attention to the care of each child.

Parents were also encouraged to take steps to improve their children's general well-being by the growing involvement of the state in providing better healthcare. The high levels of infant mortality and child ill-health had led to the gradual introduction of school meals, school medical inspection, and infant welfare. In 1905 the West Yorkshire town of Huddersfield pioneered compulsory notification of births to the Medical Officer of Health to enable a comprehensive health-visiting programme to get off the ground. Like so many of these early schemes it set out to inculcate middle-class values of thrift, cleanliness and Godliness on working-class mothers. Material aid was ruled out in favour of pious homilies on self-help, and some of the early visitors were resented for their interference. Following on from a number of voluntary schemes, the government gave financial support to local authorities to establish what became known as 'infant welfare centres'. Hundreds sprung up all over the country. By 1917, for example, Birmingham had eight municipal centres and nine voluntary centres: attendance was not compulsory and activities included weighings, advice on feeding and clothing, sewing classes, cookery demonstrations and provident clubs. Thousands of working-class mothers attended these new clinics for regular check-ups on their children's health. As a result of all these changes, coupled with improvements in housing conditions and the standard of living, the infant mortality rate plummeted. By the early 1930s it had dropped to 66 per 1000 births.

The most dramatic changes in mothering, however, came among the middle and upper classes where mothers became closely involved in bringing up their young children for the first time. They dispensed with nannies and servants in large numbers. There was a glut of 'expert' advice for them on how best to bring up their toddlers. The most popular method was that devised by childcare expert Frederick Truby King, with its elaborate, regimented and highly disciplined clock-watching routines. The aim of these routines was to improve not only the child's physical well-being but also its psychological growth. This reflected a growing understanding of child development which saw the early years of a child's life as being of critical importance to future intellectual and emotional maturity. From 1917, when Truby King set up his first Mothercraft Society at Earl's Court, his ideas became gospel for many middle-class mothers and he maintained his influence right up to the 1940s. His rigid methods of feeding were summarized in the Truby King 'bible', *Mothercraft*:

Below: Truby King childcare methods, popular with middle-class mothers between the 1920s and the 1940s, emphasized that 'breast-fed was best-fed' and that strict four-hourly feeds on the clock were essential. King's Mothercraft Society (right) ran classes which catered for the new demand for 'expert advice' from middle-class mums bringing up their own children without a nanny

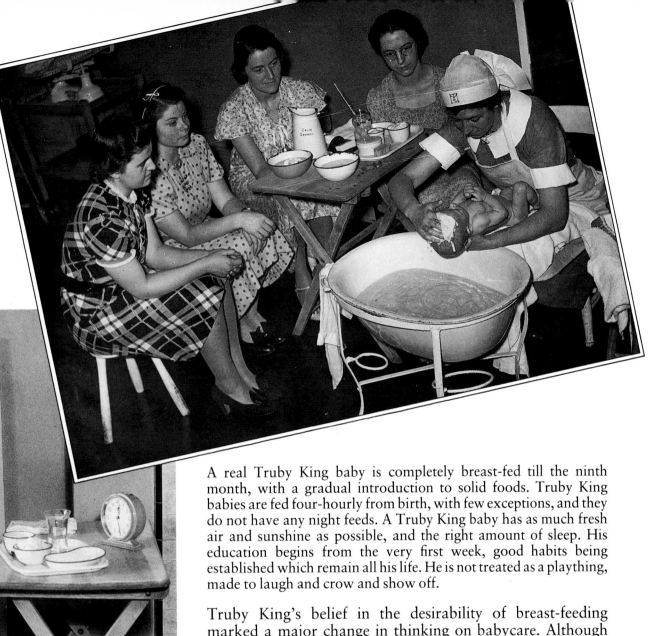

A real Truby King baby is completely breast-fed till the ninth month, with a gradual introduction to solid foods. Truby King babies are fed four-hourly from birth, with few exceptions, and they do not have any night feeds. A Truby King baby has as much fresh air and sunshine as possible, and the right amount of sleep. His education begins from the very first week, good habits being established which remain all his life. He is not treated as a plaything, made to laugh and crow and show off.

Truby King's belief in the desirability of breast-feeding marked a major change in thinking on babycare. Although most working-class mothers breast-fed their babies, the majority of middle-class mothers did not, as it was considered animal-like and demeaning. And by the 1900s more and more working-class mothers were changing to using tinned milk because it was cheap and easy. But unhygienic bottles amid unsanitary living conditions probably contributed to the high rate of working-class infant deaths. Truby King coined the phrase 'Breast Fed is Best Fed' and argued that mother's milk was cheap, natural and germ-free and exercised the baby more. Most importantly – and this was central to the new thinking on parent/child care in the inter-war period – it encouraged a closeness between mother and infant.

Dad also became more involved in bringing up the children, which often fostered closer and more informal relationships with fathers. If they were well behaved, middle-class children often enjoyed weekend treats master-minded by 'dad' like a summer Sunday motor car trip. Between 1920 and 1939 the number of cars increased from 500,000 to 3 million, most of them bought by middle-class family men. It was the age when droves of suburban families first motored out to remote spots to enjoy rambles and picnics.

And working-class fathers – enjoying a little more leisure time and, for the more fortunate, paid holidays – also came to feature more in their children's lives. The annual week-long family holiday to the seaside – a time to get to know dad – became established. Motor coaches and charabancs became a cheap and easy means of getting to the seaside. By the late 1930s 15 million people (or one in six of the population) were spending at least one week's holiday away from home. By the outbreak of the Second World War 7 million people were

going to Blackpool every year and half a million went to
one of over a hundred holiday camps in different parts of the
country. At home football grew in popularity and fathers
began taking their young sons to Saturday afternoon football
matches.

With slightly less time needing to be spent on work by both
parents and children, many working-class fathers also saw it
as their duty to help educate their children at home in the hope
that they might win a scholarship. During the inter-war years
there was a substantial increase in scholarship places available, and many fathers were keen for their children to use
education to escape from the hard life they had to endure. This
became a particularly strong tradition in many mining communities, binding together fathers with children.

Margaret Sowerbutts was born in 1923 in Trelewis,
Glamorgan, a small mining village where virtually all the
men, including her father, worked in the pit. She was the
second eldest of five children:

My mother and father both left school at twelve and had had very
little education, but there was always a tremendous number of
books around the house and my father read avidly, mainly history
and geography. And there was no question about it – we were all
expected to pass scholarship, it was called 'metric' then. Not only
were we expected to pass, but we were expected to get a credit. Each
evening, at the ages of nine or ten, we would be working in the
middle room with a nice fire with book cupboards either side. My
father would sit at the table and do the homework at the same time
as us. Then we'd all compare our answers. He wouldn't tell us what
the answers were but if we had a problem he would work it back
with us until we got it right. And it wasn't just arithmetic: he'd get a
map out and we would have to point to rivers and mountains. And
on Sundays we went for walks and he'd have little competitions
where we'd have to identify wild flowers. We got to have a great
fund of knowledge and he gave us books as presents – one year he
gave me *The Complete Self-Educator*. There was no difference in
the way he treated girls and boys, and he was quite adamant that the
boys wouldn't go down the pit.

Generally, however, it was the boys, being future bread-
winners, who were encouraged to do well at school, rather
than the girls, who were expected to do the bulk of the
housework. Sometimes talented daughters had to forgo
scholarship places so that they could be taken by sons, because
the family needed the girl's extra wage. Rhoda Dunn was
brought up in Bradford in the 1930s:

In those days the feeling was that girls didn't need educating – they weren't worth educating. They were going to grow up and go to work at fourteen and get married. Education was something girls weren't interested in. I passed twice and wasn't allowed to go but my brother went because he was the boy. I resented it a lot at the time – I felt as if I wasn't equal.

The indulgence of children – whether boys or girls – was strictly limited, however, especially in working-class families. Most families remained 'father-centred' as opposed to 'child-centred'. As the main breadwinner dad often got the pick of what food was on offer. Florence Chetwin was brought up between the wars in a village near Stoke-on-Trent, Stafford-shire:

Fathers had exalted positions in the household. My father had a special seat: the warmest seat by the fire. He had the best piece of meat or fish, and my mother cooked around what he liked. I never remember my own father making so much as a cup of tea, and he had the infuriating habit of tapping his empty cup with a spoon when he wanted a second cup of tea. He would expect one of us to jump up and pour one for him. My uncle was even worse: he would have hip-bone steak while the rest of them had stewing-beef, or on fish days he would have plaice and mother and children would have cod. He always had the first English tomato to appear in the shops, not forgetting best butter for father and margarine for the rest of the family.

Moreover, under the National Insurance Scheme, fathers were often the only member of the family entitled to free healthcare. As a result, when the children became ill they were widely treated with folk medicines and quack cures to avoid the crippling expense of paying for the doctor. This went on even as late as the 1930s. Opiates, like Godfrey's Cordial, were widely used to deal with a whole range of childhood ailments, and had the effect of heavy drugging; brown paper poultices were plastered on the chest at the first sign of a cold; and children were encouraged to find where a new piece of road was being laid to breathe in the tar fumes which it was believed were beneficial for bronchial complaints. Nellie Ingham recalls her mother's patent cures in Oldham in the 1930s:

When I had measles the light was shaded so my eyes would not be effected. For mumps mother tied a warm silk scarf around my neck. Stomach upsets were treated with a dose of castor oil or a dose of syrup of figs. For coughs goose grease was rubbed on chests. For styes on eyes the cream off the milk was smeared on. Brimstone and

This young girl in bloomers on holiday between the wars reflects the gradual relaxation of the strict rules about girls' dress

treacle was mixed and given in spoonfuls for 'clearing the blood' in spring. Mother also made beetroot and rhubarb wine for the blood. I remember an old man who came to the door selling dog-fat to rub on chests and he had a terrible cough!

The modern child-centred family arrived in full only after the Second World War. The coming of the welfare state with its free health care, combined with the improving standard of living, completed the shift in the focus of child-rearing away from survival to careful nurturing. By the 1940s there was criticism of the Truby King approach to child rearing: it was against mothers' natural instincts not to pick up a baby when it cried and feed it when it demanded it. Increasing numbers of mothers felt the enjoyment had been taken out of having children. As one critic said in a letter:

I was caught up in the Truby King Mothercraft doctrine. The health visitor prated and bullied; one's baby screamed and tears splashed down one's cheeks while milk gushed through one's jersey. But one must never pick the baby up – it was practically incestuous to enjoy one's baby.

There were fears that the method, if carried out to the letter, could severely traumatize the baby. So new ideas of nurturing, influenced by liberal theories of child care, became increasingly fashionable from the early 1950s onwards. From birth, infants would be encouraged by their parents to explore their environment and to express themselves through creative play. And with the growing affluence of the post-war years, parents could spend more and more time and money on pampering their children. Benjamin Spock's *Common Sense Book of Baby and Child Care* (1946) was bought in its millions by the new breed of mum and dad and was only outsold by the Bible. It represented a rejection of the old school of thought which stressed rigid discipline in favour of a baby which was warm, affectionate, impulsive, dependent and intelligent. By the 1950s the ideas of child psychologist Jean Piaget were also having an impact, encouraging parents to stimulate their children at defined stages of development. Crying was seen not only as a function of wetness, wind and hunger, but also of boredom. New potty-training methods, which emphasized openness, were paralleled by fun-food philosophy, which finally did away with Victorian table manners. Discipline came to be seen as a last resort: a mothercraft specialist in the April 1952 edition of *Housewife* magazine advised that 'Firmness is one of the least useful attitudes of a good parent and

A father plays with his children in Bedford, 1955. From the 1950s onwards more liberal ideas of child-rearing gave fathers a new role

certainly not nearly as important as sympathy, understanding, patience and skill.'

The new kind of child rearing still revolved around mum, but dad was encouraged to play a more important role from the earliest years, thus forging closer bonds with fathers than earlier in the century. By the late 1960s increasing numbers of fathers – most of them middle class – came to be seen as friends by their children. The most daring ones might even encourage their children to call them by their Christian names, something unheard of earlier in the century. An increasing number of fathers came to accept a slightly greater responsibility for the care of their children, in part due to economic changes: father was no longer the sole breadwinner keeping the family from starvation. More and more women were entering the job market and this was paralleled by a decline in male employment. The clear and defined roles for mother and father became blurred, and in many cases it was initially guilt as much as commitment that led to fathers from the late 1960s onwards involving themselves in nappy-changing and attending the birth. However, having done it, a few fathers re-assessed their own roles, realizing that child rearing could be enjoyable. There were even a few role-reversed families with mother as the breadwinner. But the greatest change was in attitudes towards older children who came to be treated more as equals. Parents would be less likely simply to lay down rules but would discuss with their children what they were doing and why. This resulted in an unprecedented freedom for young teenagers to stay out late and sometimes to go off on holidays with their friends.

However, by the 1960s and 1970s a new trend – that of divorce – began to undermine the more intimate bonds that were developing between children and parents. Between 1962 and 1982 there was a massive increase in divorce from just 30,000 each year to over 150,000. Sixty per cent of these broken marriages involved children, and by the mid 1980s one child in five was likely to experience divorce before the age of sixteen. Children were sometimes emotionally devastated by their parents splitting up. Angela Hogg was born in 1948 in Bristol:

My parents' was a very stormy marriage which ended in divorce in 1955. I was eight, relieved at a more peaceful homelife but very embarrassed about having divorced parents. I shrivelled in history lessons about Henry VIII when his divorces were mentioned. After the divorce my brother, sister and I were handed over to my father on neutral territory – the White Tree roundabout – every third weekend. My father then lived in Birmingham but rented one room as a base. He cooked us meals on a one ring stove but took us out to 'places of interest' – a real injection of culture! Both parents married again. It was very hard to balance loyalties. In those days nobody ever thought of counselling the children or sorting out the huge problems of being adolescents in two households. We kept our agonies to ourselves and hardly dared discuss them with each other. Things were kept much more under the carpet in those days.

More and more children had to contend with custody battles, long-running emotional tug of wars and step-parents on a scale that was unknown before the war. These children came to terms with this loss in various ways: many searched for a 'serious' boyfriend or girlfriend at a young age partly to compensate for the loss.

At the same time, the number of single mothers – often young – was increasing rapidly. By 1983 one in every eight families was single-parent with numbers increasing by around 50,000 per year. While the post-war theories on child development had emphasized the role of the father, other trends – most particularly, the breakdown in the moral and religious taboos on sexual relationships outside marriage – enabled

A 'new father' of the 1970s. With increasing unemployment and more women going out to work, some fathers began to get directly involved with babycare

women to make the choice of having children on their own. The result of both the increase in single mothers and in divorce was that by the early 1980s nearly 1.5 million children – around one in eight of the child population – were being brought up in one-parent families, the vast majority of them headed by women.

In more recent years, the role of fathers and step-fathers has been undermined further by a disturbing development – the discovery of child sex abuse. In 1987 the NSPCC alone reported 2327 cases of sex abuse (double the previous year's figures) and this was probably the tip of the iceberg. Its discovery, and the horror it now evokes, is perhaps partly a consequence of the new sensitivity to children and their rights, for there has probably always been abuse of this kind. However, its prevalence has been encouraged by the rapid growth of 'broken homes', for many of those accused of child sex abuse are step-parents. One result has been that the closeness between fathers and step-fathers and their children – encouraged throughout the post-war years – has been undermined, with fears that it may have sexual overtones. For the child victims themselves the consequences are far worse. They experience as great, or a greater, fear than those who were on the receiving end of the physical beatings common in the first decades of the century and the long-term emotional damage is deeper.

Yet despite the many problems of modern family life most children today have more friendly and intimate relationships with their parents than they would have had in the early years of the century. Smaller families, less oppressive living conditions and greater respect for children's rights and freedoms have all loosened the old authoritarian attitude towards sons and daughters. One graphic example of this is the physical affection that today's mums and dads usually show to their children. Many old people we have spoken to said their parents never kissed or cuddled them or told them they were loved. The new liberal approach to childcare has, however, brought with it new problems, even in the 'happiest' families – like power struggles with parents, disputes over bedtimes and inconsiderate behaviour. But these problems can in one way be viewed in a more positive light, as an expression of the greater independence, freedom and confidence that children today enjoy. The children of the 1980s generally seem to have more mature relationships with their mums and dads than was possible in the days when they were 'seen and not heard' and when dad's word was law.

3. OUT TO PLAY

It is part of the conventional wisdom of our time that the twentieth century, in particular television, has killed off most of the creative and imaginative games that children used to play. It is perhaps surprising then to find that folklorists and social investigators at the beginning of the century believed that they too were witnessing the death of 'traditional' children's games, untainted by commercial pressures. In 1907 folklorist Elizabeth Godfrey bemoaned the 'swift disappearance' of games like hopscotch and hide and seek, commenting 'perhaps a few who are now fathers and mothers know them – at any rate the grandmothers may; but what child of today can play them without being taught?'

Several years later another folklorist, Norman Douglas, completed a remarkable survey of children's play in the streets of Shoreditch and Bethnal Green which seemed to allay some of the worst fears of commentators like Mrs Godfrey. Douglas collected more than a thousand different games played by children in the East End ranging from tin can football to swinging on gas lamps, and meticulously catalogued them in his *London Street Games*, published in 1916. However, he too believed that these games would disappear due to the more sophisticated attractions of the picture palace and the toy industry, and the insidious influence of adult organized play. 'It all comes to this: if you want to see what children can do, you must stop giving them things. Because of course they only invent games when they have none ready made for them.'

These fears have been echoed down the century as adults have tried to engineer children's games to an ever greater extent, usually for commercial reasons or for the purposes of character formation. However, this growing adult involvement in children's world of play has not meant the death of children's imagination, nor the end of their independent games. Many of the old games live on, though sometimes in a new form. This chapter tells the story of the changes in children's play across the century: it is a story as much of the continuing inventiveness and vitality of children as of their control and manipulation.

One of the most idyllic images of children's play in the past – appearing today like a kind of paradise lost – is that of the country childhood in the time of our parents or grandparents. A host of novels and autobiographies like Flora Thompson's *Lark Rise to Candleford* and Laurie Lee's *Cider With Rosie* celebrate the richness and spontaneity of children's play in the unspoilt countryside of old England. This is often the yardstick by which the decline in children's games is measured.

Previous pages; left: children playing near Waterloo Station, London, in 1927 and (right) playing with a disused tyre in the East End in 1930. Children have always used throwaways in a whole series of imaginative games

Fishing in the Aylesbury Canal, Buckinghamshire, around the turn of the century. For country children there was much fun to be had for free

Overleaf: Blackberrying was a popular pursuit at a time when hedgerows were rich in wildlife. There were often elaborate rituals attached to games like bird nesting

There is some truth in this idyllic portrait of 'natural' play. For, despite the fact that most country children had no money and few toys, they could enjoy climbing, fishing, hunting and picking wild fruit – all for free. The migration to the cities, and decades of agricultural depression, had left a picturesque landscape with many a ruined barn and rambling hedge for children to play in. In rural areas the countryside became, in children's eyes, a great adventure playground where their imagination could run wild, building tree dens, damming streams and raiding birds' nests. Elizabeth Cornick was born in 1911 and grew up on one of the largest estates in Wiltshire where her father and grandfather were carters:

My best memories are of swinging on the low hanging branches of oak trees, and bird nesting for chaffinches' and robins' eggs among the bark of the lime trees. We played lovely games over and around corn stooks, hunting out rabbit warrens and watching baby rabbits playing. We had to watch out for the farmers and landowners though: there were big notices saying 'TRESPASSERS WILL BE PROSE-CUTED', and if they did prosecute, you didn't stand a chance because the magistrate was always a farmer too. We made our own whistles from sycamore tree branches, poking a knitting needle through the soft pulp. We whittled out bats and stumps from the trees and hedges. There was apple scrumping in the farmer's orchard, risking his riding crop around your legs. But the fields were a menace, too, when cows with calves would chase you or the old stock bull. I once

took refuge on a haystack for an hour. The farmyard took some nerve to cross: the old gander was all wings and a fearsome beak and the cock turkey once tore the front of my white pinafore to shreds. But really we didn't get a lot of time for playing, there were smaller brothers and sisters who mother told us to watch.

Some games had an elaborate ritual attached to them as Albert Mosley, born in 1899 in a small village just outside Huddersfield, explains:

You went looking for birds' nests by yourself or with your own special pal. There was a code of honour: you had to make three visits. The first time you'd watch the nest being built and then you'd go a week or two later and she'd be laying eggs. If she'd got to four eggs that was your second looking. So then you'd go the third time to look at the baby birds and then that was it. You told nobody: it was your secret where the nest was. You simply boasted. Occasionally, you'd take one egg because the birds couldn't count but you'd get belted with a razor strap if you got found out. Oh, and I remember at pig-killing time, the pig was held down and its throat was cut and when it was being cut up we lads always waited for them to throw us the bladder. We let it dry then blew it up, only no one liked to be the one to blow it up because it tasted horrible. But then we played soccer with it in the fields if we could keep it blown up.

Since most of these activities were outdoor and made use of nature's bounty, the games were often seasonal in character. There was skating and snowballing in the winter, birds nesting in the spring, swimming in the summer and conkers in the autumn. In addition, each area or even each village had its own calendar of children's customs in which mischief, dressing up and begging money often played an important part. Some of the most widely celebrated of these customs were April Fool's Day (1 April); May Day (1 May); Oak Apple Day (29 May); and Mischief Night (4 November).

However, it is easy to sentimentalize the fun and games enjoyed by village children. Often there wasn't much time for play at all. There were usually chores to do at home, younger brothers and sisters to be looked after and work to be done in the fields. Joan Hillier was one of four children and had a strict upbringing on a dairy farm in Southowram in Yorkshire in the 1920s:

It seemed I did nothing except work. It was all work and not much play. Early to bed and early to rise. Cows had to be milked before going to school and then delivered after the second milking on getting back from school in the evening. It was tea and bed by 6.30.

City children – at least those from a working-class background – also had to work and help the family, but when they
were free they too were equally imaginative in their play. Most
working-class homes were so small and overcrowded that
there was little or no space to play indoors. Parents naturally
encouraged their children to play outside in the street so that
they might enjoy a little peace and privacy – as a result the
street became the main play area. For city children the street
became a stage for a welter of running, chasing, ball bouncing
and skipping games. All these games were passed on by word
of mouth from one generation of children to another. Some of
them, like kiss-chase, relievo and British Bulldog were played
all over Britain in the first decades of the century. But there
were also strong regional variations: for example the game of
touch was widely known as 'tig' in Scotland and the North,
'tick' in the Midlands and Lancashire, and 'he' in the South
and South-East. Margaret Whitaker was born in 1906 in
Loughborough, Leicestershire, and her father was unemployed for much of her childhood:

Girls skipping in London's Shoreditch, 1922, using a piece of twine from a fruit box. Skipping was mainly restricted to girls and was often accompanied by complex rhymes and songs

66

In the spring, usually on Shrove Tuesday, we started playing shuttlecock, whip and top, marbles and cigarette cards, flipping them from the kerb edge to the house walls' side of the pavement. We also played what we called Tit Tat, which was also called Tip Cat. A short length of wood, about six inches long, tapered at each end, was hit smartly with a slender piece of wood which made it flip up and then you hit it as far as you could. Sometimes the girls would play with the boys in their games, but mostly the girls did skipping whilst the boys played whip and top. For skipping we sometimes got very long pieces which we'd stretch across the whole width of street. We played a lot of street games. Near us was a baker and his bakehouse wall was windowless, ideal for ball games and we all met there to play Sheep, Sheep Come Home.

Most city children, like their country counterparts, had little or no money to spend, so most of the toys used in their street games – for example 'go carts', which were popular from the 1900s onwards – were often made by the children themselves out of 'found objects'. Mary Brown's father was a textile worker in Halifax, West Yorkshire, and she was born during the First World War:

The games we played needed no money spent on them. For a skipping rope I used to get a rough straw rope from the boxes of oranges given away by greengrocers. These boxes had two compartments and we used them for bookcases or dolls' houses. We made dolls' furniture from matchboxes and cotton reels. We lived near the roadside and I used to copy the boys and put pins on the tramlines. When they were flattened we pushed them through bits of match sticks and said they were swords. Fussy old ladies said we'd be run over but we never were.

These children's games formed part of a children's culture which was quite independent of the adult world. Indeed, adults found many of the games annoying, anti-social or dangerous. Windows were occasionally smashed in street games; 'knock-out ginger' and many other pranks were designed to irritate adults, as one Birmingham lady recalls of her childhood:

You fixed a piece of cotton to someone's window-frame, using a drawing pin, and you threaded a button on the cotton, and took the other end of the cotton and you went out and hid in an entry. And you'd gently pull the cotton and the button would go tap, tap, tap on the window. The person would come out, see no one there and then they would go back in. And this would go on until they'd realized what was happening and then you just ran.

Opposite: Swinging on the lamp-post, 1935. Games like these were not always tolerated by neighbours or the local policeman who would often chase culprits away and give them a cuff around the ear

Right: Do-it-yourself go-carts or 'jiggers', like this one of 1908, would be imaginatively hammered together from bits and pieces. They became very popular from the 1900s onwards, much of the inspiration coming from the development of the motor car

Some games revolved around petty crime or risks on the roads and railways. This kind of play often brought children into conflict with the police, who doled out instant punishment on the street with their fist or a painful flick of the gloves or cape. Stan Gibson recalls one occasion during his childhood in the East End of London at the turn of the century, when he was punished for the crime of 'loitering':

I remember one Christmas-time we was looking in the Post Office at the top of the road, and it had Christmas goods in it. And we was looking in there, both of us; my friend and I was looking in most intently and all of a sudden, oh, we had a clip round the ear hole. It was a cold night, and the lobes of your ear was frozen and this copper – most coppers did in those days – had a knack of flicking their gloves onto the lobe of your ear. I very nearly cried of pain.

The play of middle-class children was often much more restrained than this, principally because it was controlled to a much greater extent by parents. Frequently these children would not be allowed to play on the streets; their play was much more home- and garden-based under the supervision of adults. It was often imaginative – but in a different way to that of their working-class counterparts. They played with toys, bought by parents, which often encouraged greater gender divisions than in working-class children's play. The most popular toy for boys was the toy soldier. Most girls were given porcelain dolls and dolls' houses with which to rehearse their future domestic role as mother and housewife.

A middle-class child displays her toys, 1905. Educational and 'improving' toys and books were an important feature of the nursery, where most middle- and upper-class children spent a lot of time

There was also a strong improving and educational element in the play of middle-class children, expressed most graphically in the importance attached to book-reading. This was perhaps the key feature which distinguished the spare-time activities of middle-class compared to working-class children. The better-off were often avid readers, while the children of the poor – with no children's libraries, no money to spend on books, and often no proper lighting or space to read at home – read little or nothing.

Children's literature was really created as a popular genre in Victorian times and by the eve of the First World War it was a booming industry, fashioned more or less exclusively for the children of the middle classes. However, it was the parents who invariably selected and bought the books. They could choose – on their sons' and daughters' behalf – from a host of school stories to the 'gung-ho' imperial adventures of Henty, and from the beautifully illustrated stories of Beatrix Potter to the fantasy world of J. M. Barrie – his book *Peter Pan* was a bestseller in the 1900s. Though the new breed of children's books were becoming more entertaining than in the past, they still often retained a strong moral tone and spelt out good and bad for their young readers.

This restrained, 'improving' and adult-controlled play favoured by the middle classes provided the model for a concerted effort in the first few decades of the century to get working-class children off the streets and provide them with 'character-forming' and healthy activities under the supervision of adults. This movement took a variety of forms. There were the religious inspired organizations, like the Sunday Schools and the Band of Hope, which had their roots in the Victorian period and before. They were closely tied to churches and chapels and were at the height of their power around the turn of the century. In the 1900s around 5 million children dutifully trooped off to Sunday School every week and another 3 million – often the same children – attended the Band of Hope one evening a week. At the Band of Hope children watched colourful and moralistic magic lantern shows about temperance and the evils of drink, and signed the pledge to abstain. The main motive for many children, however, was entitlement to the free annual trip to the seaside offered to those with a good attendance record by both Sunday Schools and the Band of Hope. Doris Bailey, whose father was a French polisher, was born in 1916 in Bethnal Green, East London, the second of four daughters:

Band of Hope was held every Monday evening and it attracted so many children as to need two sittings. We would queue up for about three-quarters of an hour, and the queue was so long by the time the doors opened that there would be another three hundred or so waiting to get in when we came out. Some of the children came out and tagged on to the end of the queue again they enjoyed it so much. Yet it was a very simple meeting really. We sang cheerful hymns about drinking pure water and not yielding to temptation. After that the lights were lowered and we had a story with magic lantern slides. A deep hush always settled over us as we listened to the lovely stories: nearly always about poor children living in hovels whose fathers drank away every penny. Then we sang another hymn and made for the door, taking a ticket and signing the pledge. I didn't understand the last bit, but this one thing I knew. That ticket was

my all important pass to the Christmas party. There were two excursion days a year. One was the Sunday School trip and the other was the Band of Hope, always to Southend. These two days made up the whole of our summer holiday by the sea. I loved Southend! We prayed and prayed for a fine day and with a whole shilling to spend we were millionaires for the day. We paddled and built sandcastles and crammed all our bliss into one day.

By the 1920s these religious organizations seemed very staid and old fashioned in their approach to children and they fell into decline, a decline that was particularly rapid in the Band of Hope's case. Church and chapel exercised an ever-diminishing grip on ordinary people's social life and many alternative and more interesting activities were being provided for children. Parents were less strict than they had once been in demanding that their children attend, perhaps because they believed drink was less of a social problem than it had been before the war, and the bait of the annual trip to the seaside was far less attractive to children now that the cinema was beginning to take hold.

One more modern and successful way of getting children off the streets and guiding their play, which was much favoured by early 'progressive' and Labour councils, was to build municipal playgrounds for them. Here children were provided with swings, see-saws, roundabouts, and a mass of 'ironmongery' designed to encourage safe and healthy play. The inter-war cult of fresh air and sunshine and enthusiasm

Above, left: A Sheffield Band of Hope pledge certificate. In the early years of the century 3 million children attended Band of Hope meetings every week

Opposite: London children's playgrounds in Victoria Park, Bethnal Green (above), and Bloomsbury (right). There was a boom in municipal playgrounds between the wars to encourage healthy, safe and open-air play. Adult attendants were employed to ensure good behaviour

for the great outdoors gave a massive boost to municipal provision of this sort during the 1920s and 1930s. Sandpits, paddling pools and boating lakes were often added to the array of play facilities provided for children by 'progressive' councils, like the London County Council, who encouraged kids to 'have a holiday at home'. Adult supervision was thought to be very important in encouraging 'proper' play, and children were often policed by pool attendants, park keepers and swing ladies. Most parks and playgrounds had strict 'opening hours' and the swing ladies would lock up all the playground equipment at a set time each evening. Doris Bailey remembers Victoria Park in East London in the 1920s:

There were several lots of swings, each in a well-fenced enclosure and presided over by a swing lady. She had a little hut where she would brew tea, or bandage knees, or chat with her friends, while keeping a watchful eye on the children. She was most vigilant and woe betide any rough who tried to push a small girl off a swing, or who dared to cheek her. Swing ladies were chosen for their toughness; their word was law and no one ever got the better of them. I've seen a swing lady turn everyone out and lock the gates when she saw any misbehaviour. One of our favourite games were tormenting the 'parkie' who was in charge of the little island in the centre of the boating lake where unaccompanied children weren't allowed. We'd creep across the wooden bridge and tiptoe around until we came up behind him, the king of his little kingdom, in his plain grey suit and trilby hat. 'Parkie!' we'd yell and race off in different directions. He never caught us.

Uniformed youth movements like the Boys' Brigade, the Army Cadet Force, the Boy Scouts and the Girl Guides were also formed primarily to provide character-forming play for poorer children. Boys' Brigade founder, William Smith, believed that there was a need for 'that *esprit de corps* which public schoolboys acquire as a matter of course, but which is almost entirely lacking in elementary schoolboys'. The aim was to develop qualities of discipline and patriotism in the younger working-class generation who, it was feared, were becoming lazy and degenerate, and were threatening to undermine Britain's imperial strength. As Robert Baden-Powell, who founded the Boy Scouts in 1908, put it: 'We must all be bricks in the wall of that great edifice, the British Empire.' By 1910 the Girl Guides' Association had been formed with similar aims: its handbook was called *How Girls Can Help to Build Up the Empire*.

Right: Boys square up before a boxing match in London in the 1920s. Uniformed youth movements and schools encouraged boxing among working-class children to control 'hooliganism' on the streets

Below: A Scout troop prepares to leave Waterloo Station for its annual camp, 1923. Formed in 1908 to provide character-forming play for poor children, the Scouts boasted half a million members by the 1930s

Most of these uniformed organizations achieved massive recruiting figures. In the 1930s the membership of the Boy Scouts rose to its highest ever level of almost half a million boys aged between ten and nineteen, while the Boys' Brigade boasted 150,000 members. In all, more than one in three British children passed through the ranks of one of these organizations during the inter-war years. However, their influence, though strong, was never as powerful as their founders had intended. They rarely reached the children of the very poor, or the 'hooligan' boys, as pioneers like Baden-Powell had dreamed. Many simply could not afford the uniform or were put off by the discipline and militarism. More important, if they did join it was often to be in the band or to go to the annual camp. The discipline and patriotic propaganda with which these organizations were infused sometimes were not taken very seriously at all by the recruits themselves. One parody sung by children in the 1900s went:

> 'Ere comes the Boys' Brigade,
> All smovered in marmalade,
> A tuppenny 'a'penny pill box,
> An' 'alf a yard of braid.

Perhaps most successful of all the efforts to introduce working-class children – in particular the boys – to character-forming games was that which involved organized sport. Children had played a rough-and-ready version of football, cricket and boxing in the streets and fields for centuries. What rules there were were subject to infinite local variation, and might be made up by the children as they went along. The Victorian public schools transformed traditional games like these into competitive, character-forming sports with regimented and elaborate rules of 'fair play'. The aim was to encourage qualities like discipline, courage and team spirit. From the late nineteenth century onwards ex-public school young men brought these new 'national sports' back to working-class boys through schools, brigades, churches and youth clubs. They quickly became popular and the rise of professional spectator sports, like association football – which quickly enabled gifted schoolboys to become local heroes – added glamour and excitement to these games. More and more adult supervised games and competitions featured as part of children's evenings and weekends. During the inter-war years these organized competitive sports reached their peak of popularity.

75

Even when there were no adults around, spontaneous games of football and cricket – with jackets for goal posts or wickets chalked up on walls – became one of the most popular activities for children in the street. The most dedicated would spend long hours practising their skills kicking balls against walls and such like, and dreaming of stardom. For these boys play could be a very serious business – a form of work. And for a lucky few the dream of escaping from a monotonous life down the pit or on the shopfloor by playing the game they loved came true.

The character-forming approach to children's play remained very important in the inter-war years but a new, much more brash, form of adult control, determined by commercial interests, was beginning to make an impact. Mass-produced wireless sets were bought by many parents – by 1939 nine million British families had them – and listening to the wireless became a popular family activity.

Makeshift cricket in a backstreet, c. 1930. Stumps and bails would be fashioned out of sticks or chalked on a convenient wall

'Listen With Mother', the BBC's radio programme for the under-fives, claimed over 2 million regular listeners in the 1950s

Wonderfood, the makers of Ovaltine, were the first company to use the wireless to try to influence the play of children for commercial purposes. They realized that a direct appeal to children could massively increase the sales of their 'family' drink. They broadcast a special programme for children, 'The Ovaltiney Concert Party' on Radio Luxemburg, which first went out in 1934. From it grew the League of Ovaltineys, a nationwide band of five to fourteen year olds who were sworn to drink Ovaltine loyally every night. By collecting wrappers from Ovaltine tins they could get an Ovaltiney badge, and a kit which enabled them to decipher the coded messages given out during the programme. By 1938 there were over a million Ovaltineys huddled around their radio sets noting down these secret messages which, when translated, often told them about games they could play at home or in the garden. It all encouraged a very suburban, home-based idea of play. The membership, not surprisingly, was largely restricted to

middle-class children or those from the upper echelons of the working class – if only because poorer parents simply could not afford to pay for a drink which was then regarded as an expensive luxury. Renee Smith, an Ovaltiney from Whitley Bay, near Newcastle, remembers sitting around the radio with bated breath:

My mother was a semi-invalid and died when I was eight so the radio meant a great deal to me. I had a bronze badge, then the highlight was the silver badge. For this you had to send so many labels and, as at that time Ovaltine was more expensive than cocoa, that took some doing. I think you had to enlist new members as well. The secret sign was the letter 'O' made with the thumb and first finger and the secret code was really simple: 26 letters in the alphabet so 'A' was 26, 'B' was 25 and so on. The song went:

> We are the Ovaltineys, little girls and boys,
> Make your request we'll not refuse you
> We are here just to amuse you!
> Would you like a song or story?
> Will you share our games?
> At games and sports we're all so keen
> No happier children can be seen
> Because we all drink Ovaltine
> We're happy girls and boys.

There were seven 'musts' and 'promises to do' and my punishment for not being good was not to hear the programme.

Another powerful commercial influence on children's play was the toy industry which grew rapidly in the inter-war years. The introduction of cheap clockwork motors meant that mass-produced toys were becoming much more interesting and imaginative and far less narrowly 'improving' than in the past. The market was dominated by Frank Hornby's toy empire. In 1920 he launched Hornby clockwork trains which, along with Meccano, were *the* favourite boy's toys of the period. The main toy-giving time was Christmas – itself rapidly increasing in importance as a 'play' and 'make believe' festival for children. The Christmas present trade was largely geared to middle-class children and until the 1920s most poorer children had to make do with penny toys bought from street traders, a home-made monkey on a stick or perhaps a cheap celluloid doll. However, with the rise of the cut-price chain store, like Woolworths, in the inter-war years, more and more working-class children were able to enjoy some cheaper versions of these new commercial toys. Although the more

Playing trains in the
living-room with dad
became popular from the
1920s onwards as
mass-produced clockwork
toys were introduced

expensive Hornby train sets cost around £3 in the mid 1920s
(more than the weekly earnings of many working-class families), a cheap, scaled-down version could be bought at Woolworths for seven shillings and sixpence (thirty-seven pence).
This new trend of mass toy-giving, which was beginning to get
under way, encouraged home-based, indoor play as opposed
to the traditional, outdoor pursuits which had dominated
most children's play in the past.

However, the trend towards commercialized indoor play
was temporarily halted by the Second World War. Toy factories began making tanks, and toys were strictly rationed. Many
parents and children reverted to the old DIY tradition of
making their own toys, or picked them up second hand. And
ironically the terrible destruction of the Blitz gave a great
boost to outdoor children's play. The Luftwaffe's air attacks
provided many new play areas in the heart of cities by blasting
streets and factories into bomb sites. The children of the Blitz
quickly moved in and, with a bit of imagination, the rubble
was turned into the raw material for many a new game. In
war-torn Sheffield Sylvia Land, born in 1936, played among
the bombed-out buildings:

I vividly remember playing 'chip shop' with broken slates for
fishcakes, broken bricks for fish and sand and rubble for chips. Play
shops were made out of mountains of bricks and empty cans were
threaded with precious string and formed into a loop to make
mini-stilts.

Derby was less affected by wartime bombing, but Derek Bell who grew up there recalls how the war changed his childhood games:

Street games were heavily war orientated. Most kids had toy guns made of scrap wood or similar material. In the streets were large metal canisters of oil which were burnt at night to mask the city from bombers. These made good 'cover' in a gun battle. Swapping was restricted, there were no comics or fag cards, but these were replaced by the cardboard caps from milk bottles and shrapnel, bullets and assorted metal fragments which we picked up.

In the early post-war years these bomb sites were bulldozed, and the derelict sites became a haven for exotic weeds, wild life, and most important, children's games. These patches of waste land, many of them a stone's throw from children's homes, provided a ready-made adventure playground. Terry Farrell was born in 1947 and brought up on the London County Council's Bow Bridge Estate:

A bomb-site in London's Elephant and Castle district in the late 1940s. These areas of derelict ground became havens for children to escape from adult supervision and play their own imaginative games

On the estate there were three porters and one caretaker, and these officials were supported by every kid's mum looking over the landing and controlling any games before they got too out of hand. So to escape adult prying eyes the local bombsites became the favourite private play areas. We thought they were great places to carry on our territory gang wars and to build camps. Once you were there you could spend all day with nobody to bother you. We would climb the trees, rig up rope swings, pick sides and play wars. To build camps we would use old sheets of corrugated iron, old doors, milk crates and anything else that came to hand. They were private meeting places; small fires would be built hidden from the outside world and potatoes collected from the market traders' throwaways would be cooked in the embers. I suppose the bomb sites were our countryside and gardens.

The restrictions of the austerity years continued to hold back the toy and entertainment industries for children until the mid 1950s. One sign of future trends, however, was the astonishing popularity of the radio programme 'Dick Barton Special Agent'. In 1948 it was estimated that during the winter months almost two-thirds of boys in Britain – and many girls too – tuned in to each evening episode: 1500 letters a week poured in from devoted fans. Originally it had been conceived as an adult programme, and such was the concern about its undesirable moral influence on children that questions were asked in the House of Commons, with the result that Dick's smoking, drinking and womanizing habits were severely toned down. Jean Bell was born in 1934 and grew up in Dumbiedykes, a poorer district in Edinburgh:

We never had a radio in the house until I was about twelve, then we got an accumulator-run wireless from a relative. I always remember us sitting with our ears glued to the set when the battery was running low, trying to hear the latest instalment of Dick Barton. The 'Devil's Gallop' was his theme tune and we raced in to hear him. You were always left on tenterhooks at the end until the next episode: but he always came out on top in the end!

The affluent years from the mid 1950s onwards were to give momentum to the commercialization of children's play which had taken root in the 1920s and 1930s. In 1956 the first mass craze for children engineered for commercial purposes took off: Davy Crockett, 'King of The Wild Frontier'. The success was built around the Disney film which children saw in their matinée sessions, and was backed up by a mass launch of buckskin outfits, raccoonskin caps (of which 10 million were sold) and Davy Crockett nougat bars. At the age of twelve Mary Fitzsimmons was caught up in the craze in Sunderland:

I remember the Davy Crockett craze well, making the hat out of my mother's real fur coat: she went spare, but my father was over the moon with it and wore it to the local pub. As we lived down by the docks there was a boat in and my father delivered ship orders. The captain offered my father £5 for the hat to take back home for his son. My dad wouldn't part with the hat but sharp got me making another one for the captain!

Davy Crockett captured the imagination of millions of children, but the children were far from passive victims of the 'hidden persuaders'. They incorporated Davy Crockett into their traditional games and invented a multitude of parodies, many of them adapted from the theme tune:

> Born on a table top in Joe's Café,
> The dirtiest place in USA,
> Fell in love with Doris Day,
> Thought he could sing like Johnnie Ray.
> Davy, Davy Crewcut,
> King of the Teddy Boys.

In the future children's crazes would be inspired by what they saw on the television screen – like the Hula Hoop craze of the late 1950s – as television rapidly replaced the cinema as the most popular medium of entertainment. However, not all the media-inspired crazes succeeded. Children were not easily duped and had their own likes and dislikes which were not always easy to predict. The American attempt to sell British children the crime-busting character, 'Green Hornet' – a kind of Superman figure armed with a hornet gun which fired immobilizing gas – was a spectacular failure.

In the 1950s and 1960s children became avid viewers of television, especially of children's television series like 'Crackerjack' and 'Blue Peter' produced by the BBC, or of series like 'The Adventures of Robin Hood' or 'The Lone Ranger' broadcast by the newly created ITV network. Sociologist Hilde Himmelweit's study 'Television and The Child', published in 1958, estimated that the average child was spending around two hours a day watching television. Later studies showed that children were watching more and more programmes, so that by 1970 – when colour television was well established – the average twelve year old spent nearly three hours a day in front of the 'box'. This new habit pushed back bedtimes a little, and ate into other activities like reading, homework and listening to the radio. Perhaps most important, it began to reduce the amount of time children spent playing with friends outdoors.

The puppet version of Enid Blyton's *Noddy* was one of the first children's programmes on commercial television in the 1950s. Television quickly overtook the cinema in popularity

This trend towards child television viewing was encouraged by factors other than the attractiveness of the programmes themselves, however.

A number of social developments in the 1950s and 1960s deprived children of their traditional play areas. Bomb sites were built on, increased motor traffic made play in the streets difficult or impossible, and many working-class neighbourhoods were knocked down to make way for high-rise estates where there was less space and safety for children's play. And in the countryside the play space available for children shrunk as more and more land was brought into cereal production, hedges and trees were chopped down, and farm machinery and toxic pesticides began to make the fields a dangerous place for children to play in.

People feared that television was exerting an even more sinister influence on children by robbing them of their imaginations and inventiveness and in its place planting an appetite for violence. This was often held to be one of the major causes of the dramatic rise in child crime and vandalism in the post-war years. Vandalism, in particular, became a major cause for concern: between the mid 1960s and 1970s the cost of damage inflicted was estimated to have increased about sevenfold. By 1976 £1.25 million was being spent each year on repairing vandalized telephone boxes (a favourite target for child 'vandals') alone.

The most careful studies of vandalism have noted, however, that violence on television was probably only a minor factor in

Children outside a 'prefab' in London's East End in 1959. Wartime bombing and housing shortages had broken up many old working-class communities and when families were rehoused it was often in blocks like Kelvin Flats (right) in Sheffield. They provide an horrendous example of the 1960s high-rise developments which robbed city children of their play-space

Train-spotting at Heaton Norris Junction, Cheshire, in 1955. It was a very popular hobby among boys, reflecting their increased pocket money and independence

explaining its increase: it is often only 'problem' children, many of whom already have pronounced violent tendencies, who try to emulate the violence they see on television. A more important factor in explaining vandalism is the loss of children's play space in the cities and countryside.

Yet there is a more positive – and often forgotten – side to children's play in the new era of television and affluence. Many children have had their eyes opened by television to interests and creative activities that they would never have thought up on their own. Indeed, the coming of the affluent society has enabled the majority of children to enjoy a much wider range of activities than in the past. At home children increasingly have the benefit of a room of their own where they can play with toys, read, listen to records, watch the television or pursue their hobbies. Before the war this personal space and privacy – as well as the enjoyment of 'bought' toys and books – was a luxury restricted to better off children.

The fact that modern children and their parents have more money and mobility has enabled them to pursue a greater variety of outdoor hobbies. In the 1950s and early 1960s, for example, in the last days of steam, train-spotting became all the rage among boys. The ultimate aim of the train-spotter was to collect the number of every train in Britain, which involved young boys – sometimes accompanied by fathers or teachers – travelling to many faraway cities in search of new train numbers. This provided children with a mobility and a source of adventure which would have been out of the question for most of them before the war. Pocket money was avidly saved and some train-spotters travelled as far as 300 miles a week. Ian Allen's Locospotters' Club reached 82,000 members in 1952 and sales of the ABC Locomotives books topped 50,000 copies in 1954. Such was the enthusiasm for this craze, railway officials became concerned about the lengths train-spotters would go to in order to enter forbidden sheds and get the most numbers. After two deaths at Nottingham, fearing more children might fall on to the track, they were banned for a time at popular stations like Crewe and Willesden Junction, and at Clapham Junction – the busiest, and thus the most popular, station in Britain – train-spotters were penned into a wire cage at the end of one of the platforms. On some occasions there were actually arrests: in 1952 seven spotters were fined two shillings and sixpence (twelve and a half pence) each at Derby for trespassing, while at Gateshead a juvenile court, dealing with fifteen boys, urged a ban on spotting books.

Many of the new games that children now play involve a strong element of adult supervision and control – or at least the observance of rules created by adults. There is ice-skating on the new rinks, pony-riding, five-a-side football in Sports Centres, computer games and so on. Also, the importance of bought toys has reinforced differences in play between boys and girls as commercial toy-makers have encouraged action and adventure toys for boys, and maternal and glamorous ones for girls.

This great range of pursuits and games that children can enjoy today has meant that traditional play, of the sort children make up for themselves, has lost some of its old appeal. Nevertheless, these traditional street games have survived the coming of television, motor traffic and even post-war immigration in 'ethnic' inner-city areas. In many school playgrounds today these games can be seen, still being enjoyed. A lot of ethnic children have learned and adapted the 'traditional' British games and, at the same time, contributed ones of their own, such as body-popping. The main difference is that the children who play these games are younger than in the past. Nowadays, hopscotch, skipping games and chase are rarely seen outside a primary school setting. By the time they reach secondary school, most children are enjoying a vast range of more sophisticated activities.

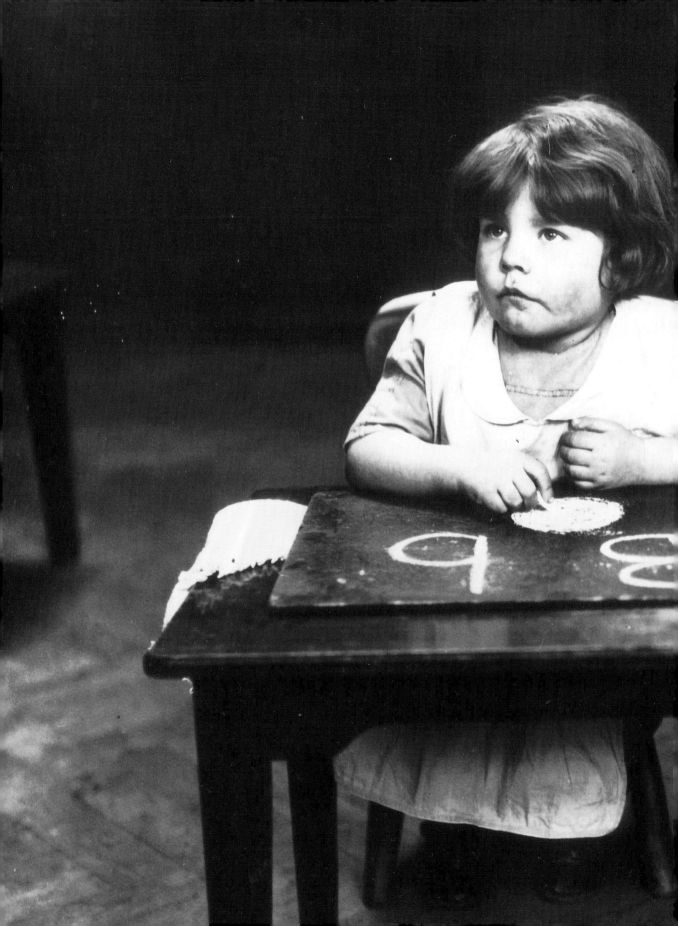

4.OUR CLASS

WE OFTEN think of schools, orphanages and reformatories as being completely different kinds of places, treating children in very differerent kinds of ways. But there are, in fact, many surprising similarities in these institutions, and they share much in common in the way they have changed in the twentieth century. All were devised as great 'character' factories, to churn out obedient and dutiful citizens for the new industrial age. The grand Victorian style of school building, in which the training was to take place, can still be seen in almost every town and village in Britain. Often circled by a high wall or fence, these buildings are a testimony to the great faith in the power of closed institutions to control children and mould young minds.

During the first decades of this century many of these institutions were extremely autocratic, and teachers – acting *in loco parentis* – frequently abused the extensive powers they enjoyed over the children in their charge. This chapter examines the strong grip that this authoritarian tradition has exerted on children's institutions as diverse as blind schools and boarding schools. And it tells the story of the growing influence of progressive, child-centred ideas, from the educational pioneers and experimental schools of the 1920s and 1930s to the post-war trend towards a more liberal and sensitive treatment of children.

The first decades of the century were the heyday of the large 'live-in' institutions for children, in which the staff assumed the role of parents. The prevalence of sickness, ill-health and poverty meant that many parents could not cope with bringing up their children, and high mortality at child birth meant that many children, left with just a father, were put into orphanages. Illegitimacy, too, added to the numbers in live-in institutions, for an unmarried mother was seldom able or allowed to keep her child. Moreover, children caught stealing or committing some other offence – even if the offence was trivial – were generally taken away from their families and placed in reformatories. Overall, at the start of the century more than 100,000 children were in orphanages, children's homes, reformatories and other similar institutions. All of these were in fact virtually interchangeable in terms of the type of children they cared for and the methods they adopted.

The staff of these institutions wielded absolute power over the children. The children's parents, even if they were alive, had no say in how their children were treated, for they were regarded as a positively bad influence. The children were seen to be in need of 'reform' and 'training', and the staff would set

Previous pages: An infants class in a Lambeth school in London in 1931. Rote learning with a slate and chalk was the norm in elementary schools until the 1950s

Firbank Scattered Home for orphaned and abandoned children in Oldham, Lancashire, in 1915. The shaved heads and folded arms vividly illustrate the harsh methods used by such institutions

about this task of character formation with enthusiasm. Strict regimes were established, revolving around early rising, cold baths, drill and, above all, corporal punishment.

Of all the institutions, the reformatories generally had the harshest regimes, marked often by brutality and cruelty. Ted Channing, born in 1901, had just turned fourteen when he was caught for stealing a bag of coal to give to his mother to heat the family home. He was sentenced to serve five years at Fulham Reformatory School, London:

I remember the matron when I arrived on me first day: she was only five foot but stiffly built. She come up to me and she hit me – punched me that side the face, this side the face, punched me everywhere! All me face was all bruised and then they shaved all me hair off, give me a cold water bath and put me in dormitory number seven. When you went to bed there was no talking, there was an orderly in the room all night, and if you said anything you'd get a belting in the morning. You had a pot under your bed but it was a crime to use it, yet it was there! In the morning at about six o'clock the whistle used to go and if you didn't get up straightaway they'd pull you out. Then you marched outside and you'd have drill to about eight o'clock then you marched into breakfast: two slices and a cup of tea. Everything was in order! If you went to the toilet you had to ask and a bloke would go with you. You couldn't blink your eye if you wasn't told to! You wouldn't believe it, mate! There was blokes in there, one was in – he'd pinched a handful of winkles – five years! It was terrible, terrible!

91

Dr Barnardo's orphans in the early years of the century. The disciplinarian regime was reinforced through stark uniforms and strict regimentation

Many inmates tried desperately to escape but few succeeded. Most were quickly arrested and returned to face a brutal public flogging. Ted Channing:

I got sixteen with the birch for trying to escape through the stoke hole when I was cleaning it out. They tied you to a gymnasium horse in front of all the lot. After about the first couple of strokes I passed out. But I remember one bloke got twenty for nicking a file from the workshop – he hid it under his tongue. So I thought I hadn't come off so bad!

The orphanages – who took in destitute and poor children as well as those with no parents – were in many ways remarkably similar to the reformatories. Although there had been attempts to create more of a family atmosphere in orphanages by, for example, introducing house 'mothers', the regimes remained harsh and disciplinarian, characterized above all by a lack of love. After his mother's death in 1914, Wilfred Chadwick was put into Firbank Scattered Home in Oldham:

They never used your name: I was number seven and we had a mother who looked after us. Ooh, she was heartless and cruel! You lived in fear. There was no love. She showed no sympathy: she should never have been in charge of children! Once I had to peel potatoes with a knife because there was no peeler and was made to eat the potato peelings because we'd cut too much off. We had breakfast at six and once it was over we were detailed a specific job to do. Every small lad had an older lad in charge of him, and if you wet the bed or if you hadn't cleaned your clogs properly you got a good hiding from him on the sly. You had to sleep with your legs straight: the mother would come up when you were asleep and throw your bedclothes back and then cane you across the legs for sleeping with your knees up. We had to do all the work in the home: we had to scrub the stone floors, mop the steps, prepare the food. Everything had to be done in a certain way. You couldn't talk, you couldn't run about, you could only read what they wanted you to read. You never laughed and if you did she'd want to know why: laughter was something you never heard. We never felt as though we were wanted.

During the first decades of this century, disabled children, too, were being drawn into harsh live-in institutions. Traditionally, mental and physical disability had been regarded as the work of the devil and it was thought that little could or should be done to help these symbols of evil. But by the turn of the century views were shifting, and disability was increasingly seen as a disease which could be treated. There was, as a

Disabled children at Peterborough Road Special School, London, in 1906

94

result, a growth in state and charitable institutions for groups like the blind and the deaf and, for the first time, the state began to intervene in the upbringing of the disabled.

Cyril Hayward-Jones, born in Shrewsbury in 1903, was blind from birth. At the age of five he was taken to the Mount School for the Blind and Deaf near Stoke-on-Trent:

It was a Tuesday when the School Board man came round and told my parents I'd got to go to school and that was that. My mother was crying and was very worried about it. It was completely out of the blue. My father took me and as soon as I got there they whisked me off down a maze of corridors into another room. Then a boy told me to undress and he was so impatient – not like my mother at all. I was fumbling a bit uncertainly and he ripped them off. There I was stood shivering and half naked and then they searched my hair and put something cold on my chest and looked down my throat. Then I was sent for a cold shower and dressed and said goodbye to my father. He kissed me goodbye and told me to be brave. I cried my eyes out that night – it was the first time I'd been on my own you see.

These new institutions were set up partly to keep the disabled away from other children, for the new and influential science of eugenics claimed that these children were of bad stock and might pollute the British race. But these special schools for the disabled were also guided by more humanitarian motives. Life was, at that time, extremely difficult if you

Opposite, above:
Modelling with clay at
Powis Street School for
the Blind, London, 1908.
Below: Disabled children
at Peterborough Road
Special School learning to
read, 1906

were disabled, and it was felt that training at a young age would help these children cope as adults in the hard world outside. To instil the necessary skills to survive, the children would be forced through a daily routine of difficult, and often painful, exercises, backed up by insensitive punishments. Cyril Hayward-Jones:

The playground had lots of posts and bars and to test our nerve and perception of sound we were made to walk around behind a partially sighted boy without touching. If you didn't listen carefully and keep behind him you'd bump into a post and I got many bruises from that. The discipline was very strict: you couldn't talk over meals. One punishment was being sent to live on the 'deaf side' for a fortnight, and of course the deaf couldn't hear and we couldn't lip-read so it was a fiendish punishment. The training was very strenuous indeed: we spent more time standing up than we did sitting down. We were being trained for a hard life – there were an awful lot of blind beggars in those days – but it was a hard way to learn.

It was not, however, just those who in some sense were 'outsiders' or 'failures' for whom institutional life was the norm. Most upper- and middle-class boys were sent away to boarding school from an early age. Although conditions were considerably less harsh than in the various institutions for the poor, these children, too, were having their character shaped in an authoritarian manner. Of course, for them the training was designed to make them 'leaders' rather than the 'led'.

From the first days in the 'prep' school to leaving their public schools, these young boys would be taught the importance of corporate loyalty and manliness. Of central importance in this process was organized games. Lord Berness, for example, observed of his time at public school in the 1900s: 'At Elmley you were made to feel that organized games were the touchstone of character: they were the ultimate criterion of failure or success.'

The rules of these schools were strict, and covered every aspect of life. The boys would be told what to wear and when, how to cut their hair, where to go, when to sleep, when to get up and when to speak. Minor infringements of the rules resulted in beatings, usually given on the backside by sixth-formers or house masters. The whole ethos stifled self-expression and individuality. At the same time, rigid ideas of hierarchy and status were instilled. At Charterhouse, for example, seniority was indicated by subtle variations in the uniform: the boys were allowed to wear coloured socks in the second year, coloured handkerchiefs in the third year and so on. And the fagging system reinforced the idea of hierarchy in, for many younger pupils, an extremely cruel and vicious way. Lord Bath, Viscount Weymouth as he was known in his childhood, was born in 1902:

I suppose the first time that I was really unhappy was when I had to leave home and go to my prep school in Kent. It was a very good school, but the discipline of course was very strong. The headmaster was a great disciplinarian. I remember whenever we played football one had to hang one's jacket on the peg which was allotted to you, and if you hadn't hanged it up properly it would fall to the floor, and the houseman or houseboy used to go round and collect them, take the name of whose it was, and give them to the headmaster. And you never knew you'd dropped anything until breakfast the next day, and the headmaster used to say 'Weymouth, you left your pants on the floor.' And you had to go up there and you had to hold out your hand. I remember so well, I mean he used to give you a hard one on each hand. It hurt like hell: it was really agonizing. The same thing went on at Harrow and the discipline there was probably more severe than it was at my prep school. There were prefects and there were fags. I, of course, was fag to a prefect. And they used to call 'Boy!' and then there was a mad rush by the two boys to get there first, and the last one had to do the job. And I remember once I was twenty minutes late from a run and the senior prefect had me up and he gave me three on my behind, very hard, which hurt like hell. They really do beat boys when they say beat. Being very thin you feel it much more. But I was never late again.

There was great faith in the power of the public school style of institution to shape children's character, and it was seen as increasingly important by those in authority for the mass of working-class children to be given a similar character-forming training through the state elementary school system. But the main working-class tradition of education was anti-institutional. Until the late nineteenth century between a third and a half of working-class children went to small, private 'dame' schools where there were no attendance registers or punishments. These 'dame' schools – named, as such, after the women who invariably ran them – allowed the children to come and go as they pleased. Most of these 'dame' schools were forcibly closed down by the state in late Victorian times. But some continued well into this century.

Of these Miss Beetlestone's in Walsall, West Midlands, was the last survivor. Operating from two neighbouring houses, Miss Beetlestone's 'dame' school was extremely popular among working-class families in the area; the number attending in the early years of this century rose to around seventy pupils. Pupils paid sixpence a week, plus a halfpenny in winter for coal, although this fee would be waived if Miss Beetlestone knew that the family had fallen on hard times. The popularity of the school – even in the face of free state schooling – centred not just on the flexibility of the school hours, but also on the fact that Miss Beetlestone herself was an exceptionally entertaining and interesting teacher. Pip West, born in 1913, was a pupil at the school for four years in the 1920s:

It was free and easy: I always say I never felt I went to school because it was like going from home to home. She was a lovely old lady, Miss Beetlestone, and we were a bit of a motley crowd. The main thing for me was that my mother needed me to help in the house, so I only went to Miss Beetlestone's in the morning and helped at home in the afternoon. And she allowed me to take my younger sister – who must have been about eighteen months old – and she just crawled on the floor in the class: no one minded. But Miss Beetlestone never used punishment and there were no desks, just tables gathered round. I was very happy there and it was certainly a change from Whitehall School, just over the road, which I went to before Miss Beetlestone's. They were very, very strict there: they'd crack you across the knuckles with a ruler for just about anything. But she taught us a lot, Miss Beetlestone; she loved children.

Despite its success and popularity, the local education authority were determined to close the school down. They were particularly angered by the fact that Miss Beetlestone was recruiting pupils from the council-run school on the other side of the road. In 1937, following a lengthy series of court actions, the school was forced to close its doors. It was the last of the working-class private dame schools, having taken in pupils for over fifty years.

In the place of schools like these came compulsory education in state elementary schools. Elementary schools taught working-class children the 'Three R's' more effectively than before and also kept them off the streets, but they were often harsh places where children were taught discipline and obedience in an authoritarian atmosphere which had no place for individuality and imagination. Iris McKenzie, who attended an elementary school in Gloucestershire just before the First World War, recalls the way that she was forced into what the teacher saw to be 'normal' and 'correct' behaviour:

Boys at Eton College in 1907. Rules about uniform were very strict and minor infringements were frequently punished with beatings

I was left-handed and Miss Ford, my teacher, made me wear a black glove and write with my right hand. She even tied my left hand on the underside of the desk. It was a set rule, you had to use your right hand. I still use my right hand for writing but I use my left for everything else.

Unquestioning obedience and conformity were enforced, above all, by the use of the cane and tawse, or leather thong. This reliance on corporal punishment created an atmosphere in which brutality could flourish. Fred Brewster, at school in Islington in London in the early years of the century, remembers:

I hated school – they put me in the craft class where they put all the idiots and people who couldn't learn. I was always getting the cane. Me hands used to be sore as hell – I used to put them on the cold water pipes. And on this particular day I was playing up: he saw me shooting some blotting paper dipped in ink with an elastic band, you know. 'Come out, Brewster, and stand behind me' and he turned round in his chair and went whack! He hit me in the earhole and knocked me right across the room and made me ear bleed. I've still got the bit of cauliflower ear that he left.

Larry Goldstone went to school in Manchester in the years before the First World War:

You see, the teachers at that time, without any doubt, were sadists. They ruled with fear. They firmly believed in the adage that kids were to be seen and not heard. All they needed was the least excuse: if you were one minute late, if you weren't sitting upright, or if you had dirty hands, they'd cane you without mercy.

The syllabus, too, would inculcate these values of obedience and conformity. Religion was at the heart of the school day, with the 'wrath of God' being regularly invoked in support of deference, hard work and discipline. Frank Unwin, born in 1906, went to a Catholic school in Liverpool:

They were always trying to ram religion down your throat. It seemed like half the day was taken up with prayers and services and religious instruction, telling you what to do and what not to do. And the teachers expected you to go to Mass on Sunday, that was thought to be part of your education. The priest would give you a ticket when you went and you had to hand in that ticket to the teacher every Monday morning. Now I didn't like it so very often I didn't go, and I got into a lot of trouble over that. Out the front I had to go and he would cane me for not having gone to Mass. Oh, that was a regular thing in my day!

Imperialism also played a major part in school life. Many elderly people remember the map of the world in every classroom: the British Empire on which 'the sun never set' would be etched out in red. Heroic national events and leaders doing battle with inferior races were an essential part of the school syllabus, and offered examples of loyalty, good citizenship and patriotic duty. Empire Day on 24 May was one of the high points in the school's calendar. Generally, the whole school would have a holiday, with celebrations and parades through town.

But the elementary schools were generally less effective at character training than were boarding institutions. The children spent less time at school, going home to parents each evening and playing in the local streets. Quite often, the children wouldn't turn up at all and played truant. And there was also greater scope for opposition and resistance to the harsh regimes inside the schools. Mothers would sometimes confront the teachers with complaints about the severity of the punishment. Generally, these confrontations took the form of verbal threats and sometimes they had the effect of curbing the worst excesses. After his particularly vicious assault on the ear, Fred Brewster's mother went round to the school:

My mum loved her kids: anyone hurt her kids and she's after them like a shot. So I went home and I told her about my whacking and she said, 'Right, I'm coming up in the morning.' Up she comes and we're in the hall doing prayers and I suddenly heard doors banging and the next minute the doors burst open and me mum come in. She said, 'Where is he? Where's the one that hit my son?' There was nearly a fight but eventually the headmaster calmed her down. It worked, though, the teacher got a warning and I didn't get clobbered quite like that again.

Occasionally the protest would become violent, erupting into near riots, as Ada Iles remembers about Edwardian Bristol:

The mothers used to come up and play merry hell with the teachers for caning us. Another thing mother'd go mad about was when we weren't allowed to go to the toilet and we ended up wetting ourselves. Our Aunt Sally'd be up there all the time, 'cause she was poor, but she never used to lay a finger on her girls, never. Once she came up and pulled the teacher's hairpins out. Then she caught hold of her hair and started to drag her out of the classroom and into the playground. Of course, we kids were enjoying every minute of it, shouting and cheering, 'Go on, have her!' And the kids in the other

Date.	Name of Child.	Age.	Offence.	Amount of Punishment.	Signature of Teacher who inflicted the Punishment
19. XII. 05	Thomas Clarke	6	same as for last three.	2 strokes	J M Lewis
" " "	George Lloyd.	6		" "	J M Lewis
	John Collinson	6.		1 "	J M Lewis
April. 3rd 06	Harry Heywood	6.	Truant playing in Ordsall Park.	3 Strokes each.	E E Smith
	Thos. Matthews	6			
	Edward Daprall	6.			
Sept. 19. 06	John Robinson	6.	Left Room ran Home. Swore & attempted to strike his Fr.	A sound good whipping & sent for parent	E E Smith

Punishment books like this one from St Clements Infants School, Salford, in 1905/6 show how even the youngest children were caned for minor acts of rebellion

classes saw what was happening and they pushed their teachers aside and ran out to join us. It was a proper riot. We were all shouting and screaming. Anyway, they got us back in eventually and Aunt Sally got summoned, fined five pounds for that.

There were also sporadic school strikes organized by the children themselves. The most significant of these strikes was the 1911 nation-wide strike staged against corporal punishment. It was a time of major industrial action all over the country, with thousands of dockers and miners striking, and the school children seem to have taken a lead from their fathers. The school strike seems to have started at Bigyn School, Llanelli, in South Wales, when pupils, incensed by a particularly unfair punishment of one of the boys, decided to take action. During September 1911, the strike spread to hundreds of schools in sixty major towns and cities throughout Britain. At Hull thousands of boys and girls toured the streets with banners demanding an end to caning. At Montrose the young strikers wanted better heating, shorter hours, no homework, holidays during potato-picking, free pencils and the abolition of the Board man. At many places, like Manchester, the pupils took their revenge on the school. Larry Goldstone from Manchester:

ANTI-CANE STRIKE.

Schoolboys at Llanelly Demand Shorter Hours and No Punishment.

A strike of infants against the exactions and sternness of nurses is brought within the limits of probability by recent events in South Wales, where they carry labour upheavals to undreamed of limits of immaturity.

The "last word" in strikes at Llanelly is a strike of schoolchildren, which still continues with "unabated vigour and bitterness on both sides."

"It's all very well," a *Daily Mirror* representative was told by one little strike leader, overseeing his pickets outside a school, yesterday. "Our fathers strike—why should not we?"

"But your fathers work twelve hours a day and you only work about four and a half," it was suggested.

"Yes; but our fathers get paid for their work; we don't. Besides which, our fathers pay for us to go to school, and the teachers cane us. That comes to the same as our fathers paying to have us caned, and we won't have it!"

"Now, then!" came a sharp voice from close by, addressing the hero. "Why aren't you in school? In you get."

And in he "got," crestfallen, and in went his followers, sheepishly enough.

A few minutes later the strikers were lined up in the school yard, receiving each in his turn "six on the hand" for being late for school.

From outside came the sounds of tumult, and a "demonstration" of well over a hundred schoolboys came in sight. They were going round visiting the different schools to fetch out "blacklegs."

According to a statement by the headmaster of Bigyn, the "strike" began on Tuesday morning last, during his absence owing to indisposition. Several of the boys, for no definite reason, according to the headmaster, left the playground and did not return to school.

The "strikers," however, obtained recognition on their return to school in the afternoon, when the headmaster, who had also returned, caned every one of them.

(Photographs on page 8.)

LLANELLY'S SCHOOLBOYS IMITATE THE ADULTS AND GO ON STRIKE.

The schoolboys of Llanelly, having, they consider, a grievance against the conditions of their "employment," have, in emulation of their elders' recent efforts, gone out on strike, and stedfastly refuse to go to school. (1) Llanelly schoolboys singing and parading the streets during school hours by way of a demonstration. (2) The loyal boys, or non-unionists—the strikers call them blacklegs—entering Bigyn-road School yesterday morning.—(*Daily Mirror* photographs.)

Left and above: The *Daily Mirror* parodies the strike of schoolchildren against corporal punishment which spread to schools all over Britain in September 1911

On the big day they met outside the school, over three hundred of them, and they marched to a field opposite the gaol walls of Strangeways. Then they marched along the main road, singing their battle parodies, and threw some stones at the school windows. The strike lasted for three days, but eventually they gave up and returned to school, and all the classes were lined up in the main hall to witness the punishment of the ringleaders as a lesson to them.

In the last resort the authorities could always get their way, and, although the excesses of the disciplinarian regimes in the elementary schools could to some extent be mitigated, these schools remained harsh places. Indeed, for those who tried to rebel against the authority of the teachers, there was the ultimate sanction of being sent to a 'training', or 'industrial', school. These institutions were set up for the children the state elementary schools could not cope with – the 'troublemakers' and the persistent truants. The threat of being sent to an industrial school was enough to keep many a rebellious pupil in order, for these schools, modelled on the reformatories, were particularly heartless places. Frank Unwin was sent to Highfields Industrial School near Liverpool during the First World War:

I hated school so I would sag off, go down the market and do odd jobs there. Well, when I was ten I sagged off for three weeks, and the attendance officer he chased me across the market and got hold of me, and the result was I was sent to this industrial school for six months. They made you feel like a prisoner, like you'd committed some great crime. You had to march everywhere; march to your dormitory, march into meals. And most of the time you weren't allowed to speak; you had to be silent practically all day – it was to break your will. Well, I couldn't stand that, because you couldn't stop me talking, so one day we had a games lesson in a field by the sand dunes and I decided to run away. They had boys and masters posted as sentries all round the field, but there was lots of long grass and I managed to crawl away without being seen. Then I ran all the way down the dunes back to Liverpool, and I lived rough in the docks for a few days. 'Course, I got hungry and I decided to come back so I marched back into the school. I was taken into the gym and the whole school was assembled. They laid me out on a table and there was a boy at each corner holding down my arms and legs. Then the headmaster beat me as hard as he could. I know I was biting my collar; I had it in my mouth so that I wouldn't show any pain. I wasn't going to cry, and he hit me all the harder because I didn't. And after that I was sentenced to another four years stay at the school as a punishment. In the end I was there longer than anybody else.

By the inter-war years, however, the institutional regimes of the past were beginning to be criticized for dealing with children in an unnecessarily harsh and counter-productive way. Progressive educational ideas, stressing the importance of learning through exploration and play, were beginning to change teaching methods for younger children. Margaret McMillan, who had pioneered improvements in child health-care through the introduction of the country's first school baths, school meals and school medical inspections, argued vigorously for such novel ideas as open-air lessons and close parental involvement. During the 1920s, thousands of young children passed through her Deptford nursery school, learning to explore their environment through the imaginative use of everyday objects.

At the same time, Maria Montessori was also emphasizing the importance of ideals, like freedom from punishment and learning through discovery. The Montessori Method, as it became known, highlighted the need for freedom of movement and the use of 'apparatus' to encourage imagination through play and manual dexterity. The most significant take-up of these ideas in the state sector came in Acton, Middlesex, where the director of education started to intro-

Above: Dumb-bell drill at Highbury Truant School, London, in 1908, and (below) shoe-shining at Upton House Truant School, London, at the turn of the century

Institutions like these aimed to impose mechanical habits of work and discipline upon rebellious working-class children

duce her methods into local schools. Wilfred Davison, born in 1921, went to East Acton School in the mid 1920s:

It was a very easy school, no discipline, and when I was ill I can remember I was sent regular picture postcards by the teachers. We learnt grammar using coloured cards: to this day I still associate certain adjectives with colour because that's how we were taught. We learnt lots of practical skills through things like lacing up shoes, and they taught us geometry using three-dimensional models. We did carpentry with real tools and wood, and made clothes on frames on the desk. We worked in small groups of about six and used the apparatus on the floor or on the table tops. We did music and dancing in our bare feet which the boys thought was rather sissy. But I'd been to an ordinary school before and I found it really enjoyable.

These first experiments were seen to be a success and in 1937 West Acton school was opened, the first-ever state school to be built using Montessori ideas as a guiding principle. Still there today, the school – with its low windows down to the ground to allow children to look out and its verandahs opening out from each class to enable open-air play – remains a testimony to the new attitudes which were eventually to sweep through the schooling system. Inside the children sat on child-sized chairs at child-sized desks, working in small groups. The teachers were seen as friends and guides rather than as dictatorial enemies, wielding canes.

In these inter-war years, the live-in institutions also started to become a little more liberal and sensitive in their treatment of children. Some of the most interesting experiments were in the special schools for the disabled being set up by charitable institutions. The National Institute for the Blind, for example, opened its first Sunshine Home for blind children at Chorleywood in Hertfordshire in 1918. The school set out to create a friendly atmosphere through its use of child-sized furniture, open areas for play and tasteful decoration. But the real innovation in its approach was the emphasis on gearing the teaching and provision to the particular needs of each individual child. In many ways, disabled schools like Chorleywood were the pioneers of child-centred education. Dorothy Hadley, born in 1918, was one of the first to go to Chorleywood, as a seven-month-old orphan:

In those days all blind children were expected to sit in a corner and do nothing – parents wouldn't let blind children do things themselves. But at Chorleywood they taught you to be self-reliant and look after yourself. We were very advanced – I could dress myself and tie my shoe laces and read braille by the time I was four-and-a-half. They used to bring things into class for us to feel so we knew what they looked like and we could get used to different things. I remember they brought a dog in and I dropped it: ooh, it was all slimy! There were lots of toys: I remember we had a rocking-horse and pedal cars. They never ever punished us: I can't remember ever being smacked. It was more or less a one to one ratio between staff and children. All the staff were very close to the children and Miss Richards more or less adopted me: she was very good to me. In fact, when I left to go to a school in Birmingham she moved with me and got a job as a teacher nearby. And she always came to fetch me and took me on trips and outings because I had no one like the other kids had. I remember years later I saw the matron and she immediately recognized me and said: 'That's one of my babies!' I think we were very precocious little whatsits really – pampered and poodled someone told us – but it was a lovely place!

Improvement in the other live-in institutions – the orphanages, the reformatories and the industrial schools – was notably slower. But even in these once overwhelmingly oppressive places change was coming. Orphans and destitute children were increasingly placed in more liberal children's homes from where they were sent to the local state school for their education. And by the mid 1930s, the distinction between the old industrial schools and the reformatories was done away with, and in their place came new 'approved' schools. With delinquency now being seen more in terms of

One of the Sunshine Homes first set up by the National Institute for the Blind after the First World War as part of a more sensitive approach to educating blind children

poor upbringing rather than simply bad character, the emphasis in these schools shifted towards trying to provide correct behaviour models for the children through leadership and example. There was less emphasis on corporal punishment as a means of improving the moral fibre and character of a child. Although the regimes were still strict, the new approved schools were considerably more humane than the old reformatories. Indeed, for some boys, these schools were now pleasant enough to be preferable to the deprivations they faced at home. John Dean, born in 1918, was in Desford Boys' Home in Leicester between 1932 and 1934:

It was a well-known fact amongst schoolboys that if you were a bad lad you could be sent to Desford. I'd heard quite a bit about it and I thought, well, Desford school cannot be any worse than what I was having to put up with at the time. My stepmother made my life an absolute misery: we weren't allowed to play out at night, as soon as we came home from school it was a slice of bread and margarine and straight to bed. When father wasn't there we got continual bashings. So I ran away from home and a couple of days later I was up before the court and sent to Desford school. I spent two years at Desford, and I'm not exaggerating when I say they were two very happy years. It was the first time I'd gone to bed at night between a clean pair of sheets and wearing a night shirt. And the first time in my life when I got three square meals a day. It was the first time I'd been allowed to play with other boys.

We were all in a house and you had a uniform. You went into breakfast at eight o'clock then you had the first parade of the day. All the boys lined up in the quadrangle in their houses and then every boy was inspected: his hands, his neck, his boots, his tidy appearance. The whole system of discipline was based on a system of order marks. Now you started off the week with six order marks and you could lose one or two for minor offences: you perhaps hadn't cleaned your boots properly or you hadn't washed the back of your neck. Now if you lost those six marks and you committed another offence you went to the headmaster who put your name in a black book. Then if you got another offence you got the cane. But the rules were all set out and followed. You felt it was more of a school than an institution.

The greatest and most 'outrageous' experiments of the inter-war years were, however, taking place outside the state system altogether – in the 'free' schools. During the 1920s and 1930s a number of influential schools were set up with the explicit aim of breaking the adult-controlled institutional regimes of the past. They saw themselves as 'little democracies' for children.

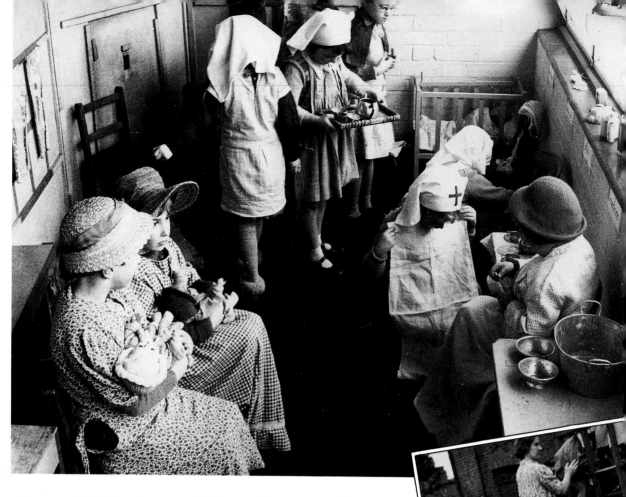

Summerhill School, set up in Dorset by A. S. Neill in 1924, was the first of these new free schools. The whole ethos of the school was based on 'freedom': there were no punishments and few rules; even lessons were not compulsory. The view was that love, closeness and personal responsibility would do away with indiscipline among children and enable them to develop naturally. Brian Anscombe was one of the first ten pupils at Summerhill when it first opened:

I'd been to three conventional schools before Summerhill and my God! What a difference – it wasn't like school at all! It was just like joining a family. There were no pressures of any kind; there was no compulsion, no fear of authority, no punishment. Freedom was the whole point. When I went I was a nervous little boy and lacked any sort of self-confidence, but we developed emotionally because we were left to ourselves. We weren't regimented – they allowed us to develop naturally and the teaching was played down. No one was sat on and we learnt because we were left alone. Lessons weren't compulsory but most of the kids went to lessons; not all, but most did. The school was run with a weekly school council meeting where everyone had an equal vote. So the kids could outvote the

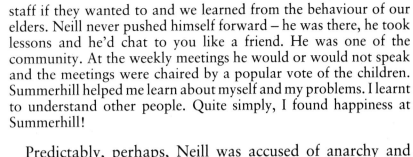

Opposite: Children dress up as nurses and tend others posing as mothers, at an infants school in 1962. This kind of role play typified the new educational ideas of the 1950s and 1960s

Below: Open-air and creative play, as pictured at this school in Tottenham, London, in the 1940s, reflected new educational ideas between the wars which emphasized learning through play and individuality

staff if they wanted to and we learned from the behaviour of our elders. Neill never pushed himself forward – he was there, he took lessons and he'd chat to you like a friend. He was one of the community. At the weekly meetings he would or would not speak and the meetings were chaired by a popular vote of the children. Summerhill helped me learn about myself and my problems. I learnt to understand other people. Quite simply, I found happiness at Summerhill!

Predictably, perhaps, Neill was accused of anarchy and irresponsibility, but his ideas were influential in progressive circles. Drawing in part on the model of Summerhill, Bertrand and Dora Russell set up Beacon Hill in Sussex in 1927. After their separation in 1932 Dora Russell carried on the school at other locations until it finally closed in 1943. Her aim was, above all, to encourage freedom of expression and thought:

We did not think it was necessarily a good thing for a child to read and become bookish and academic too early. There is a period of doing, feeling, observing the world and his fellow citizens. According to our view, freedom given and understood early enough would result in a natural evolution to maturity and self-discipline. Severity and repression of the old type almost certainly carried with it in adolescence, disturbance, confusion and the necessity for revolt.

Beacon Hill was also innovative in its emphasis on creativity and learning through art, music and dance. Dora Russell's daughter, Harriet Ward:

We called the teachers by their first names and there was a comfortable atmosphere of informality, like a large family. I remember all the lessons being interesting and pleasurable – not only the arts, which most children enjoy, but also 'hard' subjects like German and science. My mother was a Cambridge graduate in Modern Languages and taught simple French and German in the school, among other things. She had a wonderful gift for teaching small children and I still remember some of the German I learned at Beacon Hill from aged six onwards. But arts and crafts were a major part of the Beacon Hill curriculum – music, drama, dance, painting, pottery, lino-cuts, woodwork and even leatherwork, I remember. The highlights of all this were the school plays, written by the children as a collective with a teacher writing down the dialogue and stage directions, and keeping the kids' ideas within the bounds of production possibilities. Costumes were made in art classes and music worked in where needed, played by the children if possible – in fact, just like a school production at any primary school today, but in the 1930s this was revolutionary, a complete contrast to what was going on in state primary schools.

At that time, these modern ideas did not, in fact, have that much impact on the state system itself. Indeed state schools, for all the gradual change during the inter-war years, remained by and large forbidding places in which spontaneity and imagination were seen as subversive. Joyce Storey, born in Bristol in 1918, went to Two Mile Hill School in the 1920s:

The teacher wrote the word ABUNDANCE in copperplate handwriting on the blackboard and we had to copy what she had written. I loved this flowery writing. To me it was exciting and romantic. I had long since finished and was idly sitting watching the others scribbling laboriously away. The word ABUNDANCE conjured up to me A BUN DANCE and I began to draw three happy little buns complete with currants and blue bows dancing a jig. 'Tra-la-la' came a little caption out of their mouths. The paper was soon passed round and a whole series of sniggers and loud giggles followed. Then there was a voice like thunder, 'Well?' The teacher extended my stroke of genius at arm's length and after a cursory glance at it, it was torn into shreds. 'Come out here and fetch the cane,' she commanded. The burning humiliation was that you not only had to fetch your torture, you had to return it to its place afterwards. Not a foot scraped the floor, or desk banged, or a cough broke the silence as the cane was raised high in the air and then brought down hard: three strokes on each hand. I nursed my smarting palms beneath my armpits as she drew herself to her full height and told the whole class that I was a disruptive influence, a state of affairs that could not and would not be allowed to go on.

It was not until after the Second World War that progressive educational theories came to influence the state education system as a whole. The first and greatest changes were in the primary sector of education, building on the beginnings of reform in the inter-war years. Infant and junior schools became increasingly child centred, with opportunities for self-expression and creativity. Study trips and walks outside the four school walls became an important part of the new learning process. Inside school, there was also a more relaxed atmosphere, with fewer rigid rules and far less corporal punishment. From the 1960s onwards, in particular, children were encouraged to learn through play and to develop their imagination. New open-plan schools were built with desks in groups, not rows, and with room for freedom of movement. For the first time in state schools parental involvement was positively encouraged, recognizing that educational achievement was closely linked to home background and parental interest.

But for secondary age pupils, change was much slower. In both grammar and secondary modern schools, authoritarian control continued and opportunities for creativity were limited. Some of the Roman Catholic denominational schools, in particular, remained strictly regimented. Dorothy Stephenson went to a girls' convent school in Sheffield in the 1950s:

There was no talking, no running, and you had to wear your hat and your gloves in the street or you used to be reported, and then you'd be in for it! I always had trouble with the uniform and I remember once they made me kneel for three hours on the hall floor for not having a white collar: I didn't have one because we couldn't afford one. There was a great emphasis on religion: every lesson started and finished with a prayer and you had to go to church on feast days. Anyway, I rebelled and used to sneak out at lunchtime but they warned me I'd be expelled if I carried on.

In particular, corporal punishment continued to be used throughout the secondary sector to enforce discipline. Well into the 1970s the use of the cane was widespread: a survey in 1977 found that 80 per cent of secondary schools in England used corporal punishment. In Scotland, the use of the tawse was even more common: in just one term in Edinburgh schools alone the tawse was used 10,000 times. Dorothy Fraser was one of those pupils:

I remember one incident that made me very angry. We were asked by the teacher to design a new school uniform, so I drew a very trendy design complete with polo neck sweater and mini skirt. Those were the fashions that were in at the time and the other girls in the class thought it was fabulous. But when the teacher saw it I was called out to the front of the class and to my horror she produced a strap from her handbag. I was sixteen at the time and it was a girls' grammar school, so I really didn't expect this sort of treatment. Anyway, I had to hold out my hand and I got two straps on each hand. It was very painful and humiliating, and it still makes me furious to think that they could do a barbaric thing like that to me.

Due to pressure from parents' and teachers' organizations opposed to corporal punishment, the number of schools using the cane and tawse gradually diminished. It was finally made illegal in state schools in 1987, making Britain the last European country to abolish corporal punishment.

During this period state secondary schools had generally become far more liberal institutions. Comprehensives – which took over from the selective system in the 1960s and 1970s – pioneered closer and more informal relationships between

Previous pages: Nature study classes and rambles, like this one at Kingsley Green in Sussex in 1950, reflected the post-war broadening of the school curriculum

Left: Today field study is an important part of the timetable in junior and middle schools as children learn through discovery rather than by the parrot-fashion methods of their grandparents

pupils and teachers. With them came new exams and new teaching methods, both geared to encouraging the pupil to explore their environment, to ask questions and try to discover the answers for themselves rather than rigidly learning the set books of the examination syllabus. Children would, for example, go out into their local supermarkets to survey shopping patterns as part of new integrated lessons combining statistical techniques and geographical methods of analysis. Drama would be used to encourage self-expression and role-playing to explore the interpersonal relationships and problems encountered in life.

But perhaps the most dramatic changes have been in the treatment of children who would once have been put away in the harsh, live-in institutions. In recent decades, the emphasis has been on de-institutionalization and community care. Whereas in the past parents were marginalized as a bad influence, now great efforts are made to work with families, keeping children in their parental home wherever possible. And when it is not possible for a child to live with their own family, the emphasis is on fostering and adoption rather than institutional care. For disabled children, too, the emphasis is on supporting the family to enable the child to live at home rather than be taken into an institution. There was, in particular, a big move during the 1970s to integrate disabled children into their local primary or secondary school rather than being educated in separate special schools.

And for those who are still – as a last resort – sent to institutions, the atmosphere is very different from the early years of this century. The emphasis now is on affectionate bonds with adult carers rather than on authority and discipline. The Cotswold Community in Wiltshire well illustrates this new approach. This village-type community caters for severely disturbed, anti-social boys, many of whom have been in regular conflict with the law. The staff – and their families – live in this 'village', helping to create a real community feel. The corner-stone of the boys' treatment is the formation of a deep and trusting relationship with a grown-up, the aim being to counter the invariably negative experiences the children had in early childhood with a positive experience of 'parental' care. In this way, these exceptionally difficult children are encouraged and helped to develop emotionally, and the staff find that gradually the boys become less disruptive and destructive. Robert Jones has been at the community for some time:

I don't get as angry now as I used to when I first come here. I used to hit people quite a lot and start throwing things around. I took things out on things and that, and I came in and started slamming the doors and throwing things at the adults. But I like it. It's like there's a community that can help me and, well, I like the things we do here and that. The person who looks after me is Graham, he's like my key worker, and I like him a lot. The other adults are quite friendly and when they shout it's not for nothing; it's because they want you to do something. Normally they try and get us to think about what we've done and try and put it right and that, rather than punish you. They talk about it and that. There's no punishment really. But the adults, I just like them, they're like friends to me. We go out into the garden and have a laugh and play games and that. And I've been with them in meetings and things too.

Looking across the century as a whole, the treatment of today's children is a far cry from the strict, disciplinarian regimes of the past. Today young children are no longer put in forbidding and harsh institutions for the disadvantage of being born disabled or for being orphaned. They are no longer locked away from the world for begging and stealing food and fuel to survive. None of the old reformatories remain, where children used to be birched until they passed out through pain. And children at school no longer live in daily fear and dread of their teachers, worried that the slightest spark of imagination and creativity might result in the cane or the tawse.

5. FRIEND OR FOE?

THE FRIENDSHIPS children make with one another are one of the most important aspects of childhood. Yet the nature of these relationships is surprisingly uncharted. There have been few sociological and psychological studies on the subject, and even fewer historical studies. By exploring people's memories of their own childhood friendships, we have tried to fill this important gap in our knowledge of childhood this century. And the results have been fascinating. It is, perhaps, assumed that a friend is a friend, and that in any generation children will have had their 'best' friends and their close friends and their enemies. But it turns out that there have, in fact, been substantial changes in the nature and type of friendships that children make. In the earlier part of this century, children tended to form group or 'gang' friendships with strong 'tribal' loyalties. These strongly conformist, and often aggressive, gangs led to the victimization of those children who were seen as different and inferior – the weak and disabled, the poor, the illegitimate and the children of immigrants. In the post-war era, children's friendships have come to be dominated not by the gang but by the 'best friend'. In this more individualized system of friendship, there has been less positive victimization of outsiders. The new problem, particularly for the poor, is one of loneliness in a money-based society in which they cannot participate and cannot therefore form the kind of exclusive friendships that are now the norm.

The 'gang' friendships of the first decades of this century were strongest in working-class areas. The main loyalty was to the children of the street where you lived – a loyalty which was intensified by the fact that brothers and sisters would be members of the same 'street' gang. These gangs were highly territorial. Lillian Olsen, born in Edinburgh in 1920, lived in a tenement block:

In the tenements in those days they were all big families so that's where our friends stemmed from. The stairs were where we lived, and one gang would say, 'Och, you belong up there and we belong down here, so you stay to your patch and we'll stay to ours.' There'd be twelve or thirteen, maybe fourteen in our group, aged from about seven, when we could run about, up to fourteen. When our gang met we always linked our pinkies with a shake. Anyone that wasn't in our gang we'd really ignore them and tell them: 'You're not playing with us, get with your own clique.' We were quite faithful to each other, and we used to think one gang up from us were a bit snooty. We thought, 'They're too snobbish, we'll not play with them,' and they were really not much better than us. Maybe it was

Previous pages: Barefoot boys squabbling outside an eel and pie shop in London's East End around the turn of the century

Opposite: Boys, like these street urchins from the 1900s, often had a fierce territorial pride and formed gangs to protect their neighbourhood from outsiders

because their dads were clerical workers instead of manual workers, and wore a collar and tie. And they always had a decent shoe on their foot, whereas we never had. The stairhead was our clubroom and we made wee clothes for our celluloid baby dolls out of scraps of material.

The boundaries which marked out a gang's area, while often invisible to adults, were highly significant to the children. Any child caught 'intruding' on the play area of a gang of which they were not a member would be swiftly ejected. Doris Bailey, born in 1916, was brought up in the Haverfield Road area of Bethnal Green in London's East End:

Stepney, East London, in 1912. The street was the main arena for children's friendships and rivalries

Our street, being a cul-de-sac, was a favourite place for games, and there were often fights when our own gangs turned on those from neighbouring streets and told them to get back where they belonged. The Cockney fellow's street was his kingdom, and not lightly trampled on by outsiders. Even we small girls felt this bristling pride of belonging. I lived in the court, a narrow slip of a turning at the bottom of the street, and I can well remember shouting, 'Get out of our court!' whenever children from the main street came down there to play.

Just occasionally, middle-class children, innocent of the ways of these street gangs, would venture upon their territory. Ray Rochford, brought up in Salford in the North-West in the inter-war years, remembers:

The gang were out on the street one night and this grammar school boy in a peaked cap and uniform came up to us and said, 'Please can I play with you?' We couldn't believe it – it was like a baby piglet walking into a den of wolves. He had a spanking new bike. Now, we couldn't afford new bikes so we thought, 'Here's our chance.' We just started to dismantle his bike then and there. The boy cried his heart out but we didn't take any notice; we just completely stripped his bike down and he ran away. We knew the police would pick us up straightaway if they saw us riding around on a new bike, so we made three bikes out of it, putting it together with all the odd bits and pieces that we collected off rubbish tips. We thought that was a wonderful day's work. We didn't worry about the posh boy; we thought his dad would buy him another one next week to replace it anyway.

The gang would go to great lengths to ensure their exclusivity. Many had a 'badge' of identity which was known only to gang members – a particular method of greeting one another; a certain item of clothing always to be worn; a mark on the body. Billy Moore bears to this day the Indian ink mark of his childhood gang days in Sandy Row in Belfast: 'The marks were made by pricking your hands with needles and then dyeing them with the ink. It was a way of recognizing the other members of the gang when we met at the street corner.'

One of the most effective ways of encouraging an exclusive group identity was the 'secret' language. Many working-class children became remarkably fluent at their gang's language, using it to exclude outsiders from conversation and so to reinforce the sense of belonging to the gang. Sheila Ellis, who grew up in Halifax in the 1920s, recalls the special code which her gang employed:

We put the sound 'ag' before each vowel and it would go: dago yagou agundagerstagand thagis laganguagage. No one had a clue what we were talking about! We used to practise it when we were on our own and we got really good at it. We played with quite a few others and they tried it out but never stuck to it and never got as good as us! The adults couldn't understand it, and we thought we were rather clever. We got a lot of fun out of being fluent and they'd get mad.

While these gangs were territorially based – drawing their members from a particular street, tenement block or area – there were two qualities vital for acceptance into the gang: courage and physical strength. Would-be gang members frequently had to undertake dares as a sort of rite of passage into the gang. For Lillian Olsen it was jumping a dyke between the tenements without falling in; for Fred Jones, growing up in Stoke-on-Trent in the 1920s, it was walking along a high wall over a railway line; for Jimmy Cooper, in Bradford around the First World War, it was what the children called 'duffing', leaping the ten foot wide Bradford Beck. In some gangs, there was more than just one test to pass. Cyril Armstrong remembers the tests of courage he insisted on before accepting anyone into the ranks of the Top End Gang in a village in County Durham in the 1920s:

Every newcomer to the gang had to prove his worth. First they had to raid a garden and bring back tatties which we used to throw on the fire we made and eat. Then they had to knock on nine doors. They'd have to go down the road and knock nine doors in a row and if they couldn't run fast enough they'd get a sore bum or red hot ears when someone caught them. The rest of the gang would watch from a safe distance. The final test was the back street lamp-post test. None of us realized how dangerous it was. This lamp-post had an earthing strap attached to it, and we all held hands in a circle and me being the gang leader would touch this metal bracket and an electric shock would whip through the entire gang.

Even as late as the Second World War these sort of 'tests' were being used to initiate gang members. William Hughes was a young lad in Chester during these years, a member of what the local children called the 'Army' gang:

To become a member you had to stand to attention while one of the 'army regulars' – as we called them – put half a dozen or so live worms down the back of your neck. If you stood still until the last one dropped to the floor down your short trouser leg, you were in. If you moved, you were out.

The gang leaders were also chosen through tests of courage and strength. Generally, these 'tests' would centre on fights, either with challengers from within the gang or with outsiders from other gangs. At the age of fifteen, Jimmy Cooper became the leader of his Bradford gang:

There was what we called 'cock of the turn', which was to get to be leader of the gang. I never forced a fight; I was always challenged first and it amazed me how good I was. I've had yards of fights: I fought threes and fives, on one occasion eight! One time when I was a half-timer in mill I fought one lad every lunchtime for two weeks to decide who'd be cock. They used to say: 'I could gob thee,' when they challenged you.

In order for Cyril Armstrong to become leader of his street gang in the 1920s he had to take on the leader of the neighbouring Chinatown gang:

It did start in the school-yard, there was a bit of a to-do. Then the word spread, God knows who started it, and every boy and girl got the news 'Fight in Pigeon Square'. Pigeon Square was a square of pigeon huts in the allotments near to the school. Both our tempers were up and we were fighting before we got to the square and one or two others were having a go at each other as well. Once we were in the square the crowd formed a ring and we went to work on each other. He was taller than me and he put me on my back and he was walloping me; he wouldn't let me get up. Then some of the other lads started shouting, 'Fair fight, fair fight!' and they pulled us clear. Now my father was a gardener and had a greenhouse and I used to go round there and fasten the bladder of a football to the roof and use it as a punchbag. That proved my saviour because the lad didn't have a clue; he just made mad rushes at me with fists flying and I just kept out of his way and kept jabbing him. His face was a mass of blood and I kept saying, 'Pack up your bleeding!' but he kept on coming. Then, just as suddenly, he stopped, broke down crying and it was all over. My gang came over to me and that was how I really got recognized as the gang leader.

Because of this emphasis on fighting abilities and aggression, boys tended to dominate the gangs, both in terms of membership and leadership. Although many girls were members, especially girls in their pre-pubescent years, they generally played second fiddle to the boys. Margaret Traynor, born in Edinburgh in 1915, recalls: 'The boys would post us girls at the foot of the street as look-outs for the police on the beat coming, as he gave them a row for playing football.' In some gangs, the girls had a very stereotyped role, as a kind of mascot far removed from the rough and tumble and the fighting. In

Belfast, each gang would celebrate Empire Day by marching through the streets with a young girl who had been chosen to be carried along by two others girls and a boy with a blackened face. Billy Moore again:

The chosen girl was always dressed up in white and decked out in coloured paper chains and ribbons. When the queens of rival gangs met up there would be fights. And they would have a sort of competition when they met and they'd chant the rhyme 'Our Queen can burl her leg' and the rival queens would see who could do the best twirl.

But most of the day-to-day confrontations between the gangs were far more male-dominated and aggressive. Ray Rochford remembers the street battles between rival gangs in Salford during the inter-war years:

You could never venture outside your street by yourself, you'd be too frightened; you'd be chased away or just beaten up. You had your territory, and the other streets had their territory. You had to be in a gang or you were nobody. And, every so often, the word would go round that a gang from another street or another neighbourhood was coming around for a fight. Everyone armed themselves with sticks and stones and bricks. It was mostly the boys, but you'd get a few girls there in the front line. Most of them, though, were weapon carriers. You wouldn't believe the violence, it was like the Battle of Crécy. There was bricks flying everywhere, broken glass, fists flying. I was terrified but you daren't show it; if you showed yourself to be a coward your life wasn't worth living – you'd be shunned. There'd be some injuries, broken noses, broken arms. I know I ended up in the infirmary sometimes, but amazingly nobody was killed. The other strange thing was that nobody tried to stop you: the police let you get on with it and the adults watched from their windows. They must have seen it as good entertainment!

In general, many gang activities – while less violent than some of these territorial fights – would be aimed at establishing that your gang was the 'best' in the neighbourhood. One of the most common set-piece displays in which recognition could be won was the 'Battle of Bonfire Night'. In the weeks leading up to 5 November each gang would send its members out 'wooding' – or 'chumping', as they called it in Yorkshire – whereby they would compete with children from rival gangs for old boxes, branches, straw – anything that could be burned. The aim was to make sure that your gang had the biggest bonfire in the area, and the art of succeeding lay not so much in collecting the wood in the first place, but in

Crispin Street in London's East End in 1912. Working-class children spent much of their time on the streets

raiding your rivals' supplies and fighting to protect your own. Sometimes gangs would resort to setting their opponents' stores alight. In Stan Wood's village near Stalybridge, Lancashire, in the 1930s, the battle to build the biggest bonfire began as soon as the children returned to school in September:

The village was essentially territorial; it was really split into two gangs. There were the Bottom Backers at one end of the village, and the Oak Square-ites at the other. I was a Bottom Backer – of course, we thought we were the best! The rivalry was all based on the fact that our parents worked at two different mills. There was always rivalry between us and them, but it used to really flare up when we went back to school after the summer holidays. The aim was to get the biggest bonfire for bonfire night. We'd go to the mills to get wood and waste material; we'd go to the woods and get branches.

After school the main activity was collecting wood. Now, this wood was stored in secret places because you knew that your rivals would try to steal it from you. Our favourite spot was underneath the roof in the outside toilets at the back of our cottages. There was a lot of subterfuge to try to find out where the Oak Square-ites had hidden their wood. We even had girls who would be double agents and go out with Square-ite boys, just to find out secret information. In the run up to Bonfire Night there would be battles too. There would be raids on each other's stores with sticks and stones. I'm surprised nobody was seriously injured because it got very violent. One thing we'd do to protect our store was to actually hide inside our wood pile and when they came to raid we'd jump out on them and chase them away.

For upper- and middle-class children, there was nothing like street gangs, but in boarding and public schools friendships were often of a similar group nature, with physical strength and courage being very important. The loyalties often revolved around membership of a 'house' which would compete with each other on the cricket and rugby field. In many public schools, new boys and girls would have to undertake an 'initiation' ritual before they'd be accepted. At Marlborough, for example, this took the form of crawling along a red-hot radiator singing 'Clementine', at the end of which the new boys would have their faces slapped. At some schools, the boys developed special languages: at Winchester, for example, it was called 'Notions' – and boys that couldn't master this language faced ridicule or even floggings.

A disabled boy in a spinal carriage at Miles Platting, Manchester, in 1916. Many such children were excluded from gangs and street play

In a children's culture, revolving, above all, around physical ability and strength, those who could not join in were excluded from the main source of friendships at that time. The weak, the unhealthy and the disabled were, as such, ostracized from their peers. Indeed, in many working-class areas, they were often bullied, even terrorized, by the street gang. Dorothy Hadley, being blind, found her life made a misery by the children in her street in the village of Tettenhall, near Wolverhampton, in the 1920s:

I used to be frightened to go out when I came home on my school holidays, I had no friends really: I was always lonely and would have loved to have had some friends to play with. The boys used to run behind me and jump on my back when I used to go out for walks. They used to pull my hair and jump out at me to scare me. They'd call me names like 'funny eyes' and so on. I'd graze my knees and it did upset me a lot; I used to be sitting there crying. So what happened? My grandfather got me an alsatian dog. I was only eight at the time, but I had this big dog, and that did the trick. She'd give a low growl and that was enough, the boys left me alone then.

The only friendships the weak and the disabled could find were generally with girls. Although girls, and, in particular, younger girls, participated in the gangs, they were often less enthusiastic than the boys. Girls would spend quite a lot of their time, not with the gangs at all but in much smaller groups of two or three – skipping, playing hopscotch or just chatting. In this setting, the disabled would find more sympathy, at times being helped to join in. Gladys Berry, born in Sheffield in 1912, suffered from rickets:

I could not walk at all, only shuffle on my bottom. I was under the hospital's care and they tried me with splints but they were no use, and I was in a spinal carriage flat on my back for ages. I had some friends on our street and they treated me all right. In fact, my best friends used to argue over who'd wheel me to the park, and when they were skipping in the street they used to let me turn one end of the skipping rope for them. I had a best friend, Hannah, and it was her that learnt me to walk when I was ten and I started school.

However, there were some children who were excluded from friendships altogether – by both the girls and boys. Very poor children – who were generally dirty and always the most raggedly dressed – were widely discriminated against and often cruelly teased. Emma Jones, who was born in 1904, was the daughter of a sporadically employed fisherman in Grimsby:

We'd no money and I used to go knocking on doors, collecting jam jars and taking them back to the shop. Six jam jars and you'd get a halfpenny as long as they were clean! I used to have to go to pawn shop and the other kids called me 'Pawn Shop Lizzy'. I used to go down all the back streets so I didn't meet any of the school kids, because they knew where I was going and I was humiliated over that. They used to chant, 'Pawn Shop Lizzy, Pawn Shop Lizzy, we saw you taking parcels Emma,' and I daren't say much because there were too many of them for me. They always used to fight on me: they used to gang up and spit on me, and they'd get you so as you couldn't get by and then they'd pull your hair. Then they'd call you 'nitty head, nitty head' even though I never had nits.

The one consolation for such children was the fact that acute poverty was far more common than today. There were sometimes opportunities for these children to form friendships among themselves. Far greater exclusion was experienced by illegitimate children, who, being much fewer in number, would often find themselves completely isolated. During the early years of this century, the stigma of illegitimacy was immense, and children often voiced this prejudice far more cruelly than their parents. Illegitimate children found themselves rigorously excluded from friendships with other children and ruthlessly bullied. Irene Roberts was an illegitimate child, born in Lincoln in 1908. She was brought up by her grandparents, whom she called 'mother' and 'father'.

The kids used to call me 'bastard' in the streets and say things like, 'Don't go with her she ain't got no father.' I used to get in fights about the names they called me, and I never had any friends. I never got invited to a party by any of the other kids. At school the teacher used to go round the class and we would all have to say what our father did and I had to say I hadn't got a father. I had no one to talk to, and I thought my grandmother hated me because she never cuddled me or kissed me. I was so miserable when I was seven or eight, and I can remember running away to my mother but she just sent me back again.

Ethnic children – who at this time had often just arrived in many areas – were also marginalized. The period before the First World War was one of great national concern about what were thought to be high levels of immigration, especially among Jews. There were alarmist stories in the popular press about 'the foreign flood'. Major W. E. Evans-Gordon, the Member of Parliament for Stepney, voiced an all too prevalent concern when he proclaimed: 'There is hardly an Englishman who does not live under the constant danger of being driven

Len Bradbrook, the first black child in Lambeth, London, around 1910. Len suffered from being treated as a curiosity by the other children who frequently taunted him

from his home, not by the natural increase of our own population but by the off-scum of Europe.' In 1905 Parliament passed the Aliens' Act, which marked the first real attempt to curtail immigration in Britain's history. Ill-feeling and prejudice ran deep: the immigrants were thought to be dirty and overcrowded. There was a mood of xenophobia which reached fever pitch in the First World War and persisted long after.

Yet outside London and the major ports there were, in fact, few large ethnic communities: many white children had never seen a black or Asian child. Among younger children, those of ethnic minorities were often seen as objects of curiosity to be stared at from a distance. Len Bradbrook, born in 1903, was one of the first black children to be brought up in Lambeth, South London:

The neighbours used to lift up the coping of the pram to have a look at me, because there were no black babies at that time in Lambeth. My mother never liked me going out to play; she said that the other kids were too inquisitive and that it could turn to something sour. The lower type of kid would treat me rough: they used to pull me coat off me back, knock me hat off me head. And, at the same time, they'd do all sorts of horrid things – such as get hold of me and put their hands up me trousers and all the rest of it, which was a horrible thing.

When I started school my mother took my hand and took me over the road. There were about 300 children at the school and I was the only black child. I don't remember any other black child, and it was years before I saw another. Having a nice big clump of hair, which was black and curly, this seemed to appeal to the other children a terrible lot. They all wanted to grab hold of it and run their fingers through it, which was impossible. At the same time they said, 'Ooh, we'd like a head of hair like that!' They called me names: they called me 'Blackie'; they called me 'Darkie'; they called me everything they could think of. I was the first coloured child they'd ever seen. They all wanted to touch me because they wondered whether the covering – I was very dark at that time of my life – rubbed off. They thought that it was something that was added after one was born, which sounds quite stupid. And at that time it was thought to be lucky to touch a black man: some people when they saw me would spit for luck. I always responded with very great care, as my mother taught me, to be very respectful to all and then they could find no fault in me. I felt very sad for myself and I felt that I shouldn't be able to carry on if that's what was going to be my life.

Among older children, the ethnic minorities tended to be more actively discriminated against and were at times the targets of violence. In Manchester, in the years around and during the First World War, the vicious Napoo Gang terrorized the Jewish community. Originating from the Ancoats district, the Napoos were recognized by the pink neckerchief they wore and the razor blades they displayed. Most often, they would pick easy targets; young Jewish girls and women. Larry Goldstone, born in Manchester in 1910, witnessed their reign of terror:

They'd creep up behind girls and women in the street, grab the long plaited hair which hung down the back and, with a sharp pair of scissors, cut off the plaited hair and run off with it as a souvenir. They got bolder and bolder, hunting the women with plaited hair. Some used to go on the upstairs of trams late at night, and if a woman was sitting on her own, they'd cut off her hair, then, like lightning, dash off without being caught. The idea was probably hatched from the films of Red Indians scalping the whites. The tough would take the plaits to the public house to show how clever he was at hunting.

It was only after the formation of a local Jewish vigilante group that the Napoo Gang was driven out of the area and finally faded.

Yet, even during the heyday of the street gangs in the early decades of the century, there were moves afoot which were eventually to undermine the importance and even the very existence of these gangs. The authorities tended to see street gang members as 'hooligans' and were determined to get them off the street. As we saw in Chapter Three, this concern led to the massive growth of youth movements like the Boy Scouts and the Boys' Brigade. Branches of these organizations were set up all over the country. They drew in members from a far wider geographical area than just the street, and started to undermine the closed, territorial street gangs, with their hostility to outsiders. Children began to form friendships with children on a neighbourhood or district, rather than street level.

Such trends also began to change the children's loyalties. These new organizations encouraged a corporate spirit and pride. Often this revolved round organized sport. You played, for example, for the Boys' Brigade soccer team or boxed for your local youth club. These were the 'badges' of identity you now wore, and your local street gang became less important. John Williams, born in 1919, was a gang leader in Clerkenwell, in London, and 'a bit of a tearaway' when he joined the Boys' Brigade in 1928:

Emma Jones (standing)
and her sister Nellie
during the First World
War. They had got their
dresses out of pawn
especially for this
photograph

Overleaf:
The dreaded nit-nurse
examines for ringworm at
Drury Lane School,
London, in 1907. Children
found with livestock in
their hair would suffer the
stigma of segregation from
the rest of the class until
they could be treated

We were rough and tough boys – urchins really, I suppose. And it was the parties and the outings which were the main attractions to join. We'd heard about them and went along. Most of us didn't get a square meal otherwise and we'd no clothes. I led the Williams gang and we all joined at the same time – the whole gang. It was the 86th London Company and we drilled in the Smithfield market when it was shut. We used to bunk off, of course, but you needed three stars – you got a star for each attendance – to go on the outing, so you made sure you got them. My first holiday was under canvas at Hastings, and it was Captain Weaver who paid for that because I was one of nine kids and me old mum was on her own. The main BB activities were gymnasium or bands and drill, and we had swimming galas organized by the battalion where there were trophies to be won. Sometimes they'd maybe be donated by a local big-wig who was keen on the BB. You had to win the company competition, then you'd go on to the battalion competition then to the district competition. You'd get to travel all over. Our company came runners-up twice in the all-London district gym competition, which was parallel bars and apparatus mainly. And we went to play football on Hackney Marshes: we played against any other companies who'd play, and we'd change on the train or on the sidelines until some old ladies let us use their sheds for tuppence and we'd leave our kit there – not that we'd got much stuff! But it changed my way of life: it gave me a different outlook on things!

Schools, too, were gradually undermining the importance of the street gang. Like the youth organizations, they drew children from a broad geographical area and encouraged a corporate spirit. Pupils were expected to dress smartly and 'not to let the school down'. Children began to see their identity more in terms of the school and less in terms of their street gang. In many ways, this broadened the opportunities for making friends and tended to diminish the isolation of 'outsiders'. If, for example, you were weak and unhealthy, you were more likely to meet someone of like mind and body in the larger setting of the school than in your street. But there was one group of 'outsiders' for whom the values incorporated in the school ethos created greater problems – the poor. The growing emphasis on uniform and cleanliness and school image meant that those whose parents could not afford to put on a 'good show' were readily picked upon. Emma Jones:

I used to be embarrassed at school because I couldn't be dressed as nice as they were. I had this green frock – I hated it – it used to be down to me knees. My mother bought it off Ginger the rag-man; I think she gave about threepence for it. I had a pair of boots and I used to have *Telegraphs* stuffed in to make them fit. Well, you know what I'd look like! I used to be terrified when we did drill in the

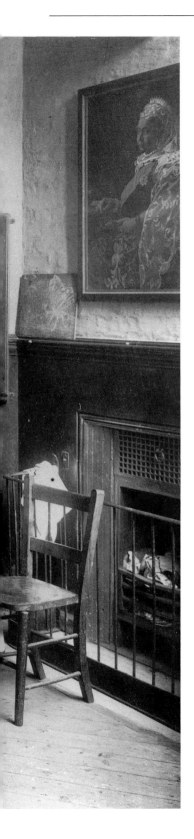

playground, in case they saw me knickers because they had nice knickers and mine were down to here with elastic in. I'd be trying to pull me frock down. Anyhow, we were very poor, and me dad, he got summoned for not paying the rates. So he was sentenced to three months in prison and that was humiliation for us. And when I went to school they all shouted, 'Your dad's gone to prison! Your dad's gone to prison!'

Moreover, many of the practices of schools – while aimed at helping the poor – often succeeded in isolating them even more. Doris Bailey remembers the visits of the 'nitty nurse' to her Bethnal Green elementary school in the early 1920s:

Every few weeks Nitty Norah would come into our classroom. She was a thin and angular woman, hair scragged tightly into a bun, with a large round navy hat firmly pulled on to her head and a starched white nurse's uniform. We would file out in silence and stand before her while the teacher sat beside her with a book. In one hand Norah held a metal comb which she dipped into a dish of carbolic. She would lift our hair, peer at our scalps and then say: one, two, or three and the teacher would write it in a book. One, we were clean; two, she was suspicious of nits; and three – dreaded three – we had livestock on our heads! After she had left the room, the names of the threes were called out, and these luckless ones had to sit alone in a separate block of desks. I had always felt a little pity for these unhappy girls. Some of them, in dirty block for the first time, would sit and cry, especially as the teacher would warn the class not to play with them again, until they were dealt with. I could not believe my ears one morning when the teacher called my name with the threes. I knew I had one, I heard her say it; and I looked frantically round the classroom with my eyes swimming. Yes, there she sat, another girl with the same surname as mine. I fought back my tears and tried to remonstrate, but the teacher only tutted. So I sat in the dirty block and shrank from everyone, trying hard not to cry. I was only seven at the time, but the memory of that morning has stayed with me all my life.

By the inter-war years, the seeds for the decline of the street gang were sown on an even wider scale. At the heart of the coming change was the rise in the middle classes. Most middle-class children had always been part of a very different pattern of friendship, based far less on being part of a group and more on close ties with particular individuals. It revolved around the idea of the 'best friend'. Most middle-class children hardly spent any time on the street, either, if they were day pupils, because they were not allowed to by their parents or because they were away at boarding school. Friendship often took place within the home. Parents would vet their children's friends, and if acceptable the 'best friend' was invited in to play at weekends or during the school holidays. Margaret Allen, born in 1892 in the Highbury district of London, was the daughter of a designer and embroiderer to Queen Victoria:

I generally used to play with my brother, and never really had any friends except a few who were the children of my parents' friends. When it was my birthday I was allowed to invite one best friend round for tea. It was always on Sunday, regardless of what day my birthday was on, and I was allowed to choose a cake. Fanny [Margaret's nanny] would organize a nice tea and a table was always put aside for my presents.

Throughout the century, it was a constant fear among middle-class parents that their children would be damaged in some way through mixing with working-class children and their 'rough' street culture. Most of the time this did not cause middle-class parents too much of a problem; cities, towns and even villages were sharply divided into working-class and middle-class districts. But sometimes the working classes got, in the view of middle-class parents, dangerously close. Action was needed to prevent intermixing. One form of defence was to build a physical barrier. In Oxford in 1934, middle-class residents on a new housing estate were so concerned that their children might be corrupted by the kids on the neighbouring council estate that they built the 'Cutteslowe Walls' across the two connecting roads. Dubbed the 'Snob Walls' they were eight feet high with vicious spikes on top. Many working-class families in the area objected intensely to the walls and, with the backing of the council, tried to demolish them. But the middle classes mounted a spirited and effective defence of their walls and it was not until 1959 that the Cutteslowe Walls were finally demolished. Joan Jones was born in 1929, and recalls the building of the wall just two doors from the council house where she was brought up as a child:

We felt cut off: it was a funny feeling really. The wall just went right across the road which we'd been used to walking along and playing along. Once it was up it was a way of life but there was lots of resentment. There were days we cursed the wall, because we had to walk all the way round and it was miles! They thought they were better than us, and we thought they'd got more money than us, which they had. At Christmas we'd walk all the way round for carol-singing and some would slam their doors. We'd play against the wall – ball or cricket or rounders – but if the ball went over you didn't always get it back. The middle-class kids didn't seem to play out as much as we did. We had gangs and played together in the road – we had each other. We didn't have the toys to play with that they had on the other side. We'd sometimes hear voices but that was it; we never played with the children on the other side. I can remember when the wall came down the first time: we jumped for joy. I can remember jumping from one side to the other shouting 'The wall's down, the wall's down!'

Excluded from the kind of street-gang life that working-class children enjoyed, the 'best friend' took on a great significance in the lives of many middle-class children. Of course, the middle classes were not the only ones to have 'best friends' but the relationships they formed with each other tended to be more intense than for most working-class children, primarily because they did not have other sources of identity and friendship through the street gang. Girls, particularly those at boarding schools, would develop very close emotional ties with their best friend – ties which would often last well into their adult life. Jill Sarsby and Liz Lucas first met at Downe House Girls' School nearly sixty years ago. Jill Sarsby recalls:

We met when we were fifteen one summer holidays when we were both in quarantine rattling around the school. We were the only two left in the school. I was in the care of about five guardians but she had her parents so I used to go up to Oban with her. Her father used to charter a yacht and we went sailing on the west coast. One year we went to Italy together. But the nice thing is that we're still very much in touch and we always pick up where we left off if we haven't seen each other for a while.

During the immediate post-war years, as a result of changes in the education system opening up grammar school places to scholarship winners, more and more working-class children were drawn into a world dominated by individualistic friendships. However, the scholarship boys and girls found they were often excluded from these friendships. The middle-class children often rejected them because of their dialect and different dress, or simply because their parents did not approve of friendships with children of an inferior social class. But these children also found they were now rejected by the working-class gangs in which they had grown up, being seen by them as 'traitors' and 'stuck up'. Kaye Winterbottom, born and brought up in the working-class district of Spotland in Rochdale, passed the 11 plus in 1954 and headed off for Bury Grammar School for Girls:

I suddenly found that the children I knew and had been friends with all my life refused to play with me and said I was snob. I was really upset and thought it was an injustice. A woman who lived nearby knocked at our front door and told my mother she'd come to let her know it was a waste of time sending girls to grammar schools, and everyone was up in arms because I was to go to a direct-grant school. When I went to Bury I found it very difficult to adapt. When I started fighting, the other girls just turned away as if in disgust. I found it very difficult to understand them. No one admired me for the things I was good at – fighting, rampaging, being wild. I broke a bottle of calamine lotion over a girl's head and was threatened with expulsion. I was forever in trouble for one thing or another. They told me I was a disgrace. Girls from Prestwich and Whitefield were from a different culture from girls from Rochdale, and we were the minority. The headmistress called us 'gals' and we had to wear a hat at all times. You couldn't speak to boys wearing it; you couldn't eat with it on; you couldn't do anything. Of course, I hated it and I refused to follow all the rules which made the posher girls angry. They had a house system – I was in Octavia Hill – but I thought it was ridiculous and just refused to have anything to do with it.

Others, too, found that as a result of new educational practices they were excluded from the children's street culture. The disabled were increasingly sent off to separate special schools, far away from the schools which most of the children on their street attended. While the disabled had always had a hard time from the street gangs, these changes tended to make them even more isolated and lonely at home than before. They became strangers in their own street.

However, the old tribal, group loyalties were by now in fast decline. The mass clearance of the inner-city slums removed the streets around which generations of children had formed their gangs. The territory which they once had defended so fiercely was no longer there. In its place arose high-rise flats with little room or opportunity for children to play collectively. Others moved out to the newly built suburbs where the traditions of the old working-class communities soon faded. Even on the 'cottage estates', like in Dagenham, or in the new towns like Harlow and Basildon, built to rehouse families from some of London's most tightly knit working-class communities, studies reveal that the children were spending more of their leisure time at home.

These working-class children began to invite their friends back home, something which would have been virtually impossible in the overcrowded housing conditions of their parents' generation. With declining family size, and improving standards of living, increasing numbers of children even

By the post-war years the gang rivalries of the earlier part of the century were gradually replaced by 'best-friendships'. This is illustrated by the number of children in pairs or holding hands in this playground pictured in 1952

had their own room. Girls, in particular, would spend hours in their room with their closest friends, cementing their friendship. Younger girls would often share an imaginative world with their best friend, known only to them. For older girls, their closeness was reinforced by confiding 'secrets' and innermost feelings with each other. Sometimes, girls would undertake semi-ritualistic vows of life-long friendship or symbolically become 'blood' sisters, by joining a drop of blood from both their fingers.

The affluence and greater mobility of the 1950s and 1960s reinforced this breakdown of street and neighbourhood friendships. Children now had the money to spend on hobbies and would increasingly make friends with children who shared the same interests. If their fellow enthusiasts didn't happen to live locally, they could afford to pop on the bus to visit or even get their parents to drive them round. Schools, too, encouraged these interest-based friendships. Most schools set up stamp-collecting clubs, chess clubs, film societies, drama groups, and many other specialist activities.

But, although the street gangs had by now largely declined, there were still vestiges of gang and group identity. One particularly important source of identity for most children was the school they went to, and often boys from one school would get into fights with boys from a neighbouring school. In the selective system of the immediate post-war years, these fights occurred most commonly between secondary modern

Building a bonfire for Guy Fawkes night: (left to right) Pakistani, Yemeni, West Indian, Mauritian and Welsh boys in Newport, Gwent, 1985. Bitter racial conflict in the 1960s and 1970s has given way to close friendships among certain second generation children

boys and their grammar school counterparts. Richard Underhill was at a Coventry prep school in the early 1950s, and remembers fights with the neighbouring Green Lane junior mixed primary state school:

The prep school boys were taunted by the primary school boys: they laughed at our uniform – we had a blazer, cap and corduroy shorts. My main rival was John Jones, and when I'd had enough I encouraged a full-scale fight between us on a bomb site near our school. I had to go home first to change out of my uniform because you got caned if you got your uniform damaged. We met at six o'clock and fought, egged on by all the other boys.

The comprehensive movement of the 1960s and 1970s tended to diminish these inter-school fights. In their place came gang fights within the school, increasingly frequently focusing on race. Between 1961 and 1966 the number of immigrant children in schools soared from 79,000 to 149,000, and children from ethnic minorities increasingly found themselves victimized, even attacked, by their white peers. The response of the ethnic 'outsiders' was to form 'gangs' themselves for self defence. They would sometimes battle it out with the white working-class children in the playground or on the streets. In this way they gradually won greater respect and began to establish their position in the communities in which they settled. Rajinder Singh, born in the Punjab in 1954, came to Bradford when he was two. At the age of eleven, he was one of the first Sikh pupils to enter his local secondary school, Belle Vue:

I had to have one or two fights to establish my credibility. And what developed were end of term fights between Asian boys and white boys, and boys coming from other schools. And I can remember vividly at Belle Vue at one time when the Asian boys had to band together and march down the road as a phalanx column to ensure their own safety. And I can also remember in 1968 things about skinheads coming to Bradford and beating up Asians and black people. There were lots of things about repatriation and leaflets going round school which were from something called 'The Yorkshire Campaign Against Immigrants'. Things like, 'If you sit next to an Asian in a class you are bound to catch smallpox.' If I look at it now I think when we were first in England we were just regarded as a kind of oddity. 'These foreign friends,' you know. And I think what happened was we just became foreign, and I think the friends bit just disappeared. There was a change in attitude so we formed an organization, the Asian Youth Movement, which was specifically designed to say 'Look, we're Asian and proud of it, and we're going to fight racism.'

139

But other groups, who had been widely discriminated against during the early years of this century, were by the 1960s and 1970s much more accepted. The biggest change was in attitudes towards illegitimate children. Even in the 1950s, illegitimate children often felt excluded from friendships. This was particularly true in rural areas where traditional values and morality held sway. Maureen Dinsdale, brought up in a small village near Leyburn in the Yorkshire Dales just after the war, felt cut off from the other children, leading an isolated and lonely childhood:

When I was young everyone in the village seemed to know about my illegitimacy apart from me. What was really my grandmother and grandfather were known to me as mum and dad. And my real mother was known to me as my sister Dot – she had me when she was sixteen. We all lived together on my grandfather's farm. The first time the seed was sown was when I went to school. I'd only been there a few days when a little girl said, 'Your mother's not your

Poor children in the slum district of Hulme in Manchester in 1954. Despite the many advances which the welfare state brought, poverty remained a problem which still deprives and stigmatizes children today

real mum.' But it was when I was seven that I really started to realize something was wrong. A boy said, 'Your Dot's your mam.' It worried me a lot and next day I faked a stiff arm to try to get off school. After that I worried about it all the time. I always felt a bit of an outsider at home; I just felt in the way. And the old people in the village used to say strange things to me like, 'How's your grandfather?' I said, 'I haven't got one.' I used to go to the barn and sit for hours and cry. And I'd go the Gill, the waterfall near where we lived, and I'd be thinking, 'Can it be true? Is my sister my mother?' over and over again. I just couldn't believe it; it seemed too awful. And I remember I used to pray to Jesus as a friend. I wanted someone to understand me and I used to pray out loud for Him to help me.

But by the 1970s, increasingly large numbers of children were being born out of wedlock. Moral attitudes had changed and illegitimate children would rarely be picked on for being 'bastards'. By the 1980s, with some three in ten children being born out of wedlock, and in some areas, such as Lambeth, almost a half, any last remnants of discrimination against illegitimate children has virtually gone.

The disabled, too, had more opportunities to join in activities with their more able-bodied peers. The educational moves which had taken these children off to separate schools were now being reversed and, wherever possible, disabled children were being integrated alongside other children in the local primary, and to some extent secondary, schools. This opened up the possibility of equal friendships between 'normal' and disabled children, in a way that was almost unknown or impossible in the past. Emma Hubbard is seven years old and has cerebral palsy: her mother explains how she has been affected by the new policy of integration:

Emma has been at Christchurch since nursery school. When it was time to go to primary school I visited some special schools, but I just didn't feel Emma would fit in. And Emma's sister was already at Christchurch Primary. So I asked the headmaster, and he said it would be fine as long as Emma could have her helper from ILEA. She loves school – she can't wait to get back to it – she hates the holidays. The other children are very good: they have a lot of patience with Emma and they have to put up with a lot, but they're good friends!

Nevertheless, the social changes of the post-war years did tend to isolate some groups more than before. This was particularly the case with the poor who, in an affluent society, were much more visible as outsiders than in the past. Poor children found it increasingly difficult to form friendships with other children in a culture that was based more and more on money and what it could buy. Apart from the stigma of being 'smellies' or 'fleabags', poor children found themselves excluded from friendships because their parents could not pay for them to have swimming lessons, Girl Guide uniforms or go on school trips, for example. Children, bombarded with advertising, were under increasing pressure to have the same toys as their friends – but in low-income families, those living on the breadline, children had to go without. With the growing division in Britain in the 1980s between the affluent majority and the poor, this has become an acute problem for many children. Mary Arnold, a single parent on supplementary benefit, lives with her five-year-old son in a small village in the West Country:

Now he's at school, and tells me about other children's bikes, and the toys they take, and holidays, and days without parents, and it breaks my heart for there is nothing for him; if he has food and clothes he can have nothing else. He has not had a birthday or Christmas present since he was two. He asks for Lego and cars from Santa, but Santa is dead in this house.

The plight of poor children highlighted a new problem – that of the child who was friendless. This was apparent on the new out-of-town estates, starved of public transport facilities, which left parents and children stranded. But it was a problem which could also affect middle-class children, whose parents moved from one area to another and who found it difficult to hold on to friends. These children were often very lonely and spent much time at home by themselves, often immersed in technological play like video and computer games.

But overall the new kinds of friendships children were forming meant that there were fewer 'outsiders' than in the days when gangs dominated the street. The increase in importance attached to individual friendships meant that most children were likely to find at least one good friend, even if others rejected them. With group loyalties weakening, the ostracization of 'outsiders', which was so common in the pre-war period, became less important. This has led to an increasing tolerance between children and an acceptance of 'difference'. Most notably, children from ethnic backgrounds have become more integrated, and while there are still some racial fights in Britain's inner-city schools, there are at the same time many close friendships between black and white children of a sort that would have seemed unimaginable just a generation ago.

Greater affluence and home-based play has caused a rapid decline in the street gang culture. More and more children now play with best friends in rooms of their own

6. THE END OF INNOCENCE

Previous pages:
'Teeny-bopper' fans in
London in 1975 hoping for
a glimpse of their idol,
Donny Osmond

Opposite: Two
photographs taken on the
same day show William
Rushton of Bury,
Lancashire, aged three, in
1920. He changed into his
first pair of red breeches
at the photographers. Well
into the inter-war years
many boys, especially in
the North, were dressed as
girls until being 'breeched'
at the age of three or four

THERE IS a sense in which children today appear to have lost the innocence we have come to associate with childhood and are more 'grown up' than they used to be. This is because they have more interest, knowledge and experience of sexuality – traditionally a key area in defining maturity – than they did in the first half of the century. Gender divisions – at least in terms of appearance – have also emerged at a very tender age. It is, above all, this growing sexualization of the world of childhood that has led to fears that we are witnessing the disappearance of childhood. Many feel that in this commercial, fashion-conscious age, boys and girls are so preoccupied with how they look and dress that they can no longer enjoy mucking about and having fun – that they are missing out on the pleasures of childhood. And people worry even more that nightly exposure to soap operas and dramas on marital failure, adultery, teenage pregnancies and promiscuity have perverted children's views of the world and given them too much knowledge at too young an age. This chapter explores the sexualization of childhood from the innocence – and ignorance – of the past to the more worldly wise child of today. It looks at the changes in girls' and boys' roles from the days of tom-boys to the traumas of boyfriends. And it asks whether the essence of childhood is threatened by this supposed end of innocence.

In the early years of this century, one of the over-riding concerns among both the middle and working classes was to postpone any sexual interest or identity in children. The main way of 'protecting' children from the opposite sex was simply to segregate them as much as possible. Parents in overcrowded working-class homes, where as many as a dozen might be sharing two or three rooms, went to incredible lengths to prevent brothers and sisters from ever seeing each other naked while dressing, washing and bathing. This was undoubtedly to prevent sexual awareness, but it is also possible that, with so many adolescent children sleeping together, parents were terrified at the possibility of incest. Fred Brewster was born in 1911 and grew up one of an extended family of fifteen in Islington, North London:

We always had that amount of respect for the sexes, you know. I can't never remember my sisters taking their clothes off in front of me, or me taking my clothes off in front of my sisters. When we had a bath we used to boil the water up in the copper out in the little lobby at the back, and when it was hot we had a tin bath in the kitchen. Three or four of us used to have to bath in the same water. One night it would be the boys' turn, and the next night it would be the girls' turn and the boys had to stay out the way. That's one thing my mother taught us: to have respect and not probe, be decent about it, you know.

Once at school, boys and girls were rigorously kept apart. There would be separate schools, or at least separate entrances and separate playgrounds, often surrounded by high walls or fences to prevent fraternization. This segregation was enforced even more rigidly in institutions for disabled children, who were often encouraged not to have relationships with the opposite sex at all for fear of reproducing what was seen to be 'bad stock'. Cyril Hayward-Jones went to a special school for the blind and deaf in Stoke-on-Trent in the years before the First World War:

We never had any contact with the girls except in prayers, they were absolutely separate from us. There was what we called the 'separation door' and there was tremendous enthusiasm for trying to talk to the girls through the door. The headmaster tended to interpret the most innocent things as signs of guilt. When a boy was seen talking to a girl, he thought it was some sort of intrigue and he took a very serious view of it. I remember once when I was fourteen I met a girl (she was sighted) at chapel. Her name was Muriel, and we spent a little time together, and I decided to write her a letter. I wrote it in braille and I was going to dictate it to one of the housemaids – she'd write it for me, you see. I remember it ended 'your passionate admirer'. I'd only seen the girl once! Well, I left this letter hanging around and a member of staff found it and, of course, I was called before the headmaster. He asked me did I kiss the girl and he wanted to know all the details. I think he got a certain sexual pleasure out of it himself. He was very cross with me; he threatened to expel me and said I was 'an unmitigated blackguard'. He said it was 'the foulest record in the annals of the school', that was for kissing a girl! I was so innocent I didn't know one end of a girl from the other. He sent for my father and I remember my father saying, 'Work, work, my son, and regain the confidence of your masters.'

In their determined efforts to maintain rigid moral standards, teachers would use physical punishment if boys and girls were caught talking, ogling, exchanging love letters or, worst of all, kissing. Reg Summerhayes, at school in Bath in the early years of the century, recalls: 'The girls' school was next door to ours and they caught I kissing a girl through the railings. I had four cuts of the cane for that.' There was even more severe punishment for being caught alone with a girl, as Bill Phillips, who went to a school in the East End of London in the 1920s, found out:

Boys enjoy a separate entrance at Myddelton School, Clerkenwell, London, just after the First World War. Boys and girls were kept apart as part of adult attempts to avoid the mixing of the sexes and to postpone the development of sexual interest

I got this girl behind the shed. 'Course, I didn't know what sex was – it was just feeling one another sort of thing. And I got caught behind the shed by the master and he had me in front of the class and he said, 'Right, I'm going to make an example of you.' He said, 'I'm going to stop this once and for all.' And he took me in the room, took my trousers down, bare backside, and caned me, and I couldn't sit down for a week.

Generally, however, boys were treated with greater leniency than girls. The school authorities – always fearing that a girl who 'misbehaved' might become pregnant – went to great lengths to instil in girls the necessity for chastity and modesty. Girls who were thought to be trying to make themselves more attractive – by dressing up or wearing jewel-

lery — were severely chastised. This was particularly true in Catholic schools. Lil Hemmings was at St Nicholas of Tolentine Convent School in Bristol during the First World War:

My father sent me a bracelet from Germany. Anyway, I was doing my sums and this nun came round, Sister Lucy, and she said, 'What's that you've got on your wrist?' 'Oh,' I said, 'it's my dad's birthday present that he sent me over from Germany.' 'Take it off,' she said. Now, we were three storeys up and our classroom overlooked the boys' playground. She took it off, opened the window and threw it out. You could tell how I felt. Anyway I ran out the class crying and I climbed right over the railings, over to the boys' playground, and got it, and she was down there waiting for me at the gate. And she belted me, she took it away again. I never had it back.

Out of school, too, girls were expected to uphold higher standards than boys. While it was generally accepted that boys would go 'larking' about, such behaviour from girls was deemed immoral, even wicked. Throughout the first half of this century, parents laid down strict rules as to where their daughters could go in the evening and what time they must be in. These restrictions were imposed on girls throughout their teenage years, and often beyond. Mary Young was a teenager in Bristol in the 1930s:

Girls' class in a state school in 1908. Even stricter rules governed the behaviour and dress of girls than that of boys

A girls' cricket match at Rugby in the 1920s, reflecting a new enthusiasm for 'unladylike' activities and outdoor games

I was never allowed to have a boyfriend and was allowed two nights a week out. I had to be home by nine in the evenings sharp or else. I had a few casual boyfriends when I was eighteen but mother always terminated them. She was very strict and very Edwardian in her ways and ideas. I abided by them and never dared to answer back or defy. But between the ages of eighteen and nineteen I became rather fond of my girlfriend's brother. We met secretly on my nights out and eventually love blossomed. But unfortunately a neighbour saw us together and told my mother. I received a severe thrashing with a cane and was stopped from having my two nights out for two weeks and was told what would happen if I didn't give up my boy.

In middle- and 'respectable' working-class families, parents' permission had first to be gained before a boy could take a girl out. Grace Sykes, born in 1899, remembers how at the age of sixteen she had her first date:

I'd met this boy in a London park and he'd ended up by asking me if I'd go out with him to a musical on the Saturday. Well, I was never allowed out after half-past eight at that time. So I said to him, 'Good gracious, no.' He said, 'Not the first house?' Because there used to be two houses from seven till nine and then from nine till eleven. So I said, 'Good gracious, no. My father would have a fit if I asked.' Do you know what he did? He wrote to my father. I thought I was in for a good wigging. Dad came down to breakfast one morning and he said, 'Grace, I want to speak to you in my study.' Into his study I went and he said, 'I've had a letter from a young gentleman called Hargrave.' So I thought what a cheek what's he writing to you about? He said, 'When a gentleman approaches me in a gentlemanly manner I treat him as a gentleman.' And apparently he'd written to ask dad if he could take me out to the Music Hall, to the first house in the evening. And I said, 'Can I go?' So surprised. He said, 'Yes. I've told your mother to answer it, providing he fetches you and brings you home.'

There were few opportunities for girls and boys to meet without this kind of prior vetting. The main one in working-class districts was the 'monkey run' on a Saturday night. Boys and girls would promenade up and down certain streets of the town, or through certain parks, in groups of three or four, hoping to 'click' by catching the eye of one of the opposite sex. A separate meeting, often as a foursome, would then be arranged, but the relationship rarely got beyond a peck on the cheek. Sex was hardly even contemplated, and in any case there was little opportunity, given that many monkey runs were closely policed. Generally, the girls and boys involved in monkey runs were in their mid to late teens or even in their early twenties. Very few children of fourteen or under would join in, and those who did were thought to be unusually precocious. The older promenaders would frequently send them home. Lucy Thirkhill was born in Bradford in 1908: her father, a textile worker, was very strict:

There was nowhere for us to go on Sundays when I was in my early teens. So, on a Sunday afternoon, we'd go to Sunday School, and then after Sunday School we'd go in Bowling Park, and all the lads used to stand down each side of the Promenade, and the lasses used to walk up and down, you know, and they used to look across. And you'd say to your mate, if any lads looked at you, you know, twice, you'd say, 'Here, I think we've clicked.' And we used to go and they used to call us across and we'd go to talk to them, and oh, it were lovely! Sometimes they'd say could they see us at night, and they'd just take us for a little walk, and then take us home. And that's all there was in it, you know. And then on Sunday night we used to go promming on Bankfoot and it were crowded with lads and lasses, crowded! They were stood in gangs were the lads and we'd be walking slowly up and down, and everyone were jostling one another!

But, although these contacts between boys and girls were invariably innocent, the fear of what might develop if boys and girls were allowed to mix freely ran deep. As a consequence, most leisure activities were, like school, strictly segregated. The formation of the Girl Guides is a good example of

Some of the first Girl Guides at camp around 1910

the concern to keep boys and girls apart. When the Scouts were formed by Baden-Powell in 1908, large numbers of girls wanted to become members. There was great enthusiasm at that time for energetic, outdoor activities, getting away from the dirty and unhealthy cities, and the girls couldn't see why they shouldn't join in. In a number of places, girl scout packs were formed going on joint rambles, hikes and camps with the boy scouts. At the first Scout rally, held at Crystal Palace in September 1909, about twenty girl scouts marched with some 11,000 boys. Among these girl scouts was twelve-year-old Sybil Canadine who recalls how they got there:

My mother used to run a jumble sale in a very poor part of South London, and I began to see that there were boys in a new kind of uniform who were going off to have interesting afternoons on Peckham Rye. It seemed to me an awful pity that there weren't any girls attached. So I asked the leader if he couldn't have some girls as well. 'Oh no,' he said, 'it's only for boys.' 'Couldn't the girls do the same things?' 'Well,' he said, 'I suppose they could.' Then I wondered whether my schoolfriends would be interested in having fun and games on Peckham Rye every Saturday. I asked the scoutmaster: 'Could we not follow at a distance and do the same things as the boys?' And so about twelve of us got together in the summer of 1909 and on Saturday afternoons off we would go, following the boys at a discreet distance. We had a wonderful time. We weren't in uniform but we learnt tracking and stalking. We took poles with us – broom handles we used. We jumped over railings and small streams. We took an old frying pan and some very ordinary, rather cheap, food – one egg or a piece of cheese and some bread – and we cooked our tea and made a fire. Then we heard there was going to be a Scout rally. We had no uniforms and no money, but we were able to borrow shirts and hats from the scouts who were not going to the Crystal Palace rally. So in September 1909 we set off to walk the six miles and we got laughed at in Dulwich village and whistled at. We'd no tickets but we made a line and, looking neither right nor left, we marched straight through without being challenged. A bit later on we were having our few sandwiches when a figure detached itself from the crowd and came towards us. We realized it was Baden-Powell himself. We quickly made a line and he came up and spoke to us and said, 'And what the Dickens do you think you are doing here?' We replied, 'We want to be girl scouts.' 'Oh, you can't be – it's only for boys.' A terrible moment for us; we thought he was going to send us away. So we gathered round him and said, 'Please, please, something for the girls.' I think the Girl Guide movement was born then, because, after a pause, which seemed the longest minute in the world, he said, 'I'll think about it, I'll let you know.' I think he had decided then that there would have to be a movement in which girls could take part.

At the first Boy Scout rally at Crystal Palace in September 1909 a handful of defiant girl scouts gatecrashed in borrowed uniforms. Sybil Canadine is seen fifth from the right

However, these girl scouts provoked great hostility. It was quite unheard of for girls and boys above the age of puberty to socialize freely with one another. One worried mother, a Mrs Violet Markham, wrote to *The Spectator* in December 1909:

The Girl Scouts and Boy Scouts roam the countryside together on what I can only describe as glorified larking expeditions, expeditions from which they have been known to return home as late as ten p.m. Girls and boys are finding their way home often in a state of very undesirable excitement. The whole spirit of excitement and self-advertisement bred by the movement is highly objectionable, and from what I have seen myself I cannot too strongly deprecate the tone and temper it creates among children at a difficult and impressionable age.

The solution was segregation, and in 1910 Baden-Powell's sister, Agnes Baden-Powell, formed the Girl Guides, a separate organization with quite separate activities. In the years that followed, the Girl Guides, with the opportunities it provided for hiking and camping and strenuous activities, proved to be extremely popular and, by the inter-war years, some 100,000 girls had become members.

This was, in many ways, the heyday of the 'tomboy'. Girls could climb trees, enjoy rough and tumble street games and excel at sports at school, without fear of being ridiculed or rebuked. The view – so prevalent among the middle and upper classes in the Victorian era – that girls should behave in a 'ladylike' way, as preparation for their role as wives and mothers, was in decline. The benefits of the outdoor, healthy life were increasingly emphasized and recognized to apply to all. And, of course, the censorious attitudes to girls who dressed up and made themselves more feminine, created an atmosphere in which girls who mucked around, looking a sight, were accepted, if not always approved of. The upshot was that girls, who were by now increasingly freed from the constraints of having to do the chores at home, could behave like boys.

The interest of girls in adventure, as opposed to romance, was reflected in, and reinforced by, the children's literature of the period. Angela Brazil's stories, first written around the First World War, were immensely popular among school girls in the 1920s and 1930s, depicting girls getting up to all sorts of daring exploits and wild adventures. Brazil girls were 'rosy, racy, healthy, hearty and well-grown' and, above all, assertive. But the most influential children's writer of all was, of course, Enid Blyton. Writing from the late 1930s onwards, she captured the imagination of a generation of schoolchildren with her stories of young adventurers solving mysteries in the face of danger. Significantly, her young adventurers included girls as well as boys, Georgina (George), in Blyton's series of books about 'The Famous Five', was a tom-boy hero, a role model for many a schoolgirl in the 1940s and 1950s.

As a result of these changing attitudes and influences, girls could be seen in many a park and back street running about wild, up to much the same pranks as the boys. Joyce Storey spent her childhood days in the village of Kingswood, near Bristol, in the 1920s:

I think I was a proper tom-boy. I spent all my time swinging through the trees, catching tiddlers in jam jars, and sliding down slopes on my backside. Many's the time I've come home with my pants dirty or ripped and been told off by mum. We had one game, it was a test of bravery, and I was always the bravest – even the boys couldn't do it as well as me. We had a long rope that we tied to a tree and we lit a bonfire near it. You had to swing on the rope over the fire and land over the other side. Some of the boys were too frightened and they couldn't get enough momentum to push themselves over but I was always good at that. That was one of the best games we played.

Many girls were simply not interested in having 'boyfriends' – indeed they would have been rather shocked and surprised at the idea. And the boys, while they might want to 'lark' around, teasing the girls, were certainly not keen to be lumbered with a 'girlfriend'. Indeed, many boys actively spurned girls, seeing boys who befriended girls as 'sissies' – in Yorkshire 'ladlasses' – to be ridiculed. Well into their mid, or even late, teens, most children formed close relationships only with children of the same sex.

This asexual view of childhood was reflected in the children's dress of the period. Children's clothes were designed to distinguish them, at a glance, from adults, and hence from the sexuality attached to the world of adults. Most boys wore short trousers, which came into vogue during the inter-war years partly as a result of the rise in the importance of scouting and sports at school. And the day-to-day clothes of girls were generally chosen to be practical rather than attractive: while girls still wore dresses rather than trousers, they tended to be loose tunics, unadorned and unstylish.

Many of those brought up during these years look back nostalgically on this era as a time when children could be children. There was a simple innocence to childhood which allowed boys and girls to play at childish games and adven-

Tom-boy George (centre) of Enid Blyton's 'Famous Five' from *Five Go Adventuring Again*. As girls took up hearty and healthy outdoor activities, fictional characters like George became role models

tures without worrying about how attractive they looked or whether anybody 'fancied' them. Girls, in particular, benefited from a shift in attitudes which put aside the stereotypes of femininity and allowed girls to relax and enjoy themselves.

But, along with innocence went ignorance, and even those who look back nostalgically on this era recognize that, for many adolescent children, this brought problems. During the first half of the century the vast majority of children knew virtually nothing about sexual matters and were often completely ignorant of the the facts of life well into their late teens. At home any mention of sex was taboo: as late as 1949 a survey by Mass Observation found that over 80 per cent of children had received no sex education from their parents at all. The most innocent remark or horseplay about sex would be quickly jumped on and punished by parents. Emma Jones was born in 1904 in Grimsby:

We used to reckon to play mothers and fathers. And I was supposed to be having a baby so I put a pillow up my dress and my mother caught us and she said, 'What are you doing?' and I said, 'I'm pretending to have a baby.' Ooh, I got the biggest good hiding I'd ever had: she used to do it on your bare bottom with a strap. No, you never spoke about anything like that. I never knew anything about sex. I was with me sister and this other girl one day and we was talking and I said, 'Do you know where babies come from?' She says 'Yes, out of the belly button.' 'Oh,' I said, 'I think it's dirty don't you? I'm not getting married if it's like that.' Anyhow we were whispering in the bedroom and me mother heard us and she gave us a good hiding and told this girl's mother and she got a good hiding too. Me mother never explained, never!

For girls, in particular, the onset of puberty could be traumatic. Many had no idea what was happening when their periods started; some thought they were dying or that it was a punishment from God. Most mothers made no attempt to prepare their daughters for menstruation, while those who did tended to pass on a feeling of shame and a sense that periods were unclean. Sanitary towels were not in general use by working-class girls, who at best used pieces of rag or sheeting. Doris Wright was born in Halifax in 1909, and was on holiday at her aunt's when she had her first period:

I was about eleven or twelve and I went into a field with my friend where there was a lot of small white turnips. We ate lots of them and went home, and next morning I started to menstruate for the first time. I rushed down to my auntie and told her it was due to all the turnips we had eaten. She said I was all right and not to worry, but

Overleaf: Bath-time in Manchester in the 1940s. Sex was taboo in working-class families and mothers went to great lengths to segregate brothers and sisters, especially on bath nights

my mother never told me anything. When my bust started growing I felt these lumps and I went to my elder sister, but she just laughed and said she would tell my mother I had been playing with lads. When I was at school a girl asked me if I knew where babies came from. I said the doctor brought them and she laughed at me. I went home and asked my sister and she said she would tell my mother and she would smack me. So I didn't ask anymore. I knew what made a baby and they were in your stomach, but when it came to me to have my first baby I waited for the midwife to cut my stomach. I honestly didn't know where he was coming from.

For Connie Denby from Sheffield, who grew up in the 1920s, the experience was even more riddled with myth and nonsense:

Menstruation started when I was ten years old. I had never even heard of it. My mother just said it was something women had to put up with and I got a verbal rocket for starting at ten instead of fourteen, which was the normal time. I was forbidden to speak about it, even to my young friends, and especially not to boys. I had to keep away from boys when like that, and hadn't to get my feet wet. I would die if I trod on cool linoleum! And that was my sex education! I'd been told that my mother's midwife had a cupboard full of babies and, as I was the bonniest, my mother picked me!

Nor was school any more helpful in imparting the facts of life. Sex education was simply not a recognized part of the curriculum in any schools until as recently as the 1960s. The London County Council, for example, banned sex instruction in 1914, and this ban was not lifted until the 1950s. As a topic of discussion, sex was taboo in school; even biology lessons steered well clear of the subject. Although there was a movement during the 1930s to raise awareness about sex it was in the context of hygiene. The National Council for Combating Venereal Disease showed a series of films with titles such as *The Girl Who Doesn't Know*, and *Damaged Goods*. These carefully avoided clear explanations in favour of warnings of the dire consequences of promiscuity, and only tended to make younger people more confused and guilty about their sexual feelings. At some schools – particularly those where religion was important – children were often taught to be deeply ashamed of their sexuality. In convents, for example, girls had to bath under a towel or in their pants and were told it was a sin to look at their own body. The writer Margaret Nevinson was rebuked at her convent school for not wearing a chemise in the bath. 'But no one can see me,' she protested. 'God sees all,' she was told.

For boys, the onset of puberty was somewhat less trau-matic. But, even so, the taboos and ignorance of these decades left many boys feeling deeply confused and guilty during their adolescent years. Nathan Stone, the son of a blade grinder, grew up in inter-war Sheffield:

When I was thirteen I had a very funny sensation. I got a slight burning sensation in my little willie. I wondered what was the matter so I went to the lavvie, which was outside in the backyard and shared by two families. I touched my willie and it started to grow. I kept on touching it and it started to spit at me. I looked at the gooey result and felt sick as a pig and dirty all over. Then the door opened and my mother came in. She seemed to know auto-matically what was happening, gave me a clip on the earhole and said, 'Nathan, that'll send thee blind if tha does it too thisen too often.'

Masturbation was seen, at the time, as immoral; a danger not only to the individual but to the whole race. Teachers, doctors and parents alike saw it as the 'scourge of the human race', as a secret sin which had seriously damaging effects on mind and body. Baden-Powell, for example, warned boy scouts in the association's handbook, *Rovering to Success*, that masturbation 'cheats semen of getting its full chance of making up the strong manly man you would otherwise be. You are throwing away the seed that has been handed down to you as a trust instead of keeping it and ripening it for bringing a son to you later on.'

These dire warnings do not appear – from the very little evidence which is available – to have stopped boys mastur-bating. But they undoubtedly caused worry and anxiety, and often a deep sense of shame, as Lord Bath, born in 1902, recalls:

My mother was a very religious woman and she wasn't prepared to say very much about the facts of life except to say that sometimes little boys did things to themselves which were rather horrible and drove them mad. In the end they went mad by playing about with themselves. I didn't know what she was talking about in those days, but I thought I shall go mad. Ludicrous! I felt that I was the only boy in England who did this terrible thing. But I couldn't stop. Then when I went to Oxford there was the Bursar and he used to have all the new boys up at Christchurch and then would talk to them. And I remember him saying to me, he said, 'Tell me, how often do you masturbate?' I said, 'Never.' 'Look,' he said, 'I think you must have misunderstood me. How often do you pass yourself off?' I said 'Never. Never, Sir.' I was so ashamed you see. I thought it was the worst thing in the world to do. He said, 'Well, you're only the second boy that I've spoken to that has come up to this college who's never done that thing.' I can't tell you what a relief it was. I felt that I'm not going to the lunatic asylum, that I'm a normal boy, and quite happy. It was the biggest relief I've ever had in all my life. In fact I began to talk about sex more than I ever did before, as though it was the normal thing to do.

For many children their innocence and ignorance was brought to an abrupt end by entry to work. On the factory floor, dirty jokes and stories of sexual adventures proliferated, and most new recruits faced an initiation ritual involving a strong sexual element. For many twelve and thirteen year olds – some of them out from school on a half-time basis – their experiences were often shocking and humiliating. Ted Harrison began work in the East End of London at the age of thirteen in 1915:

I went to work in a warehouse and I'd only been there a couple of days when a load of the young blokes got me in the corner and started to pull my trousers down. I called out but the foreman didn't take any notice. I think he was in on it because they did it to all the new boys. Well, they got my cock out and they greased it and massaged it, then they put horse shit on it and rubbed it in. It was horrible, quite a shock really, but you accepted it and when the next new boy came you were there doing it with the rest of them.

For some, the end of their innocence was far more traumatic and disastrous. In particular, girls who entered work as domestic servants were vulnerable to sexual advances and abuse. Violet Dann entered service with a wealthy family in Whitley Bay in 1929:

Every morning I had to be up at six o'clock to put the fires on; in those days there wasn't central heating. This was so the master could have his bath at eight o'clock. I'd been there about three or four months and I'd go and fill his bath up. I was in there one day and was bending over to test the water and he came in and shut the bathroom door. And he slid the bolt on it. Well, in my innocence I didn't know what was going on and he pushed me up against the window frame and he started mauling me and that. So I said, 'Is the water suitable, sir?' and he says 'That's quite alright, leave it as it is.' And he was mauling me all over like and then all of a sudden he picked my frock up and did what he wanted to do. Well, he took my pants down and had sexual intercourse. I knew it was something that shouldn't be done, but I didn't understand about things; nothing was ever explained – what happened about sexual intercourse, babies or anything.

This combination of innocence and ignorance among children – with its accompanying advantages and disadvantages – held sway for the first half of this century. But from the 1920s and 1930s onwards, new influences – which would in the end lead to a revolution in attitudes and behaviour – were beginning to arrive. The seeds of a commercial culture, dominated by the mass media, were being sown, and while the impact at this stage was primarily on adults, the effect on children was soon to follow.

Hollywood films, in many ways, marked the start of these new influences. Cinema-going was immensely popular among young adults in the inter-war years and these new, glamorous stars became the models on which behaviour and dress were based. Young teenagers of thirteen, fourteen and fifteen idolized stars like Tyrone Power, Joseph Cotten, Margaret Sullavan, Joan Crawford and Loretta Young, and tried to emulate their style. Odette Lesley, who grew up in London in the inter-war years, like many girls of her generation, went to great lengths to achieve a touch of sophistication:

Hollywood had an enormous influence on all our lives. From about nine I was absolutely avid: we went to Cricklewood and the best seat in the house was one and ninepence and there'd be an 'A' film, a 'B' film, a newsreel and a cartoon. Alice Faye was one of my favourites: she had blonde hair and deep blue eyes and a low husky voice which we'd imitate. We'd do our hair like hers – shortish in curls – and wear off-the-shoulder dresses like hers. We'd wear pure silk stockings which were gorgeous. You'd try to speak like her: we used corny lines from the films and even imitated the way they walked. I fancied myself as a singer and tried to sing like them. I always thought one day I'd go to Hollywood and be discovered! It was Judy Garland I identified with most: I laughed and cried with her over the years! And I had an enormous crush on Spencer Tracey and had fantasies about him for years. I'd fantasize that I'd meet him and have a long love scene. We heard all the film music at the dances and you were dancing with Tyrone Power or Joseph Cotten, and you'd close your eyes and let your imagination run wild! It was the glamour that attracted us. We knew the stories were unrealistic but we loved them!

In trying to capture these adult and sexualized looks, girls risked the disapproval of their parents who were brought up in a generation when children looked like children. Often these experiments with make-up and fashion would be done secretly and furtively. Florence Chetwin was a young teenager in the early 1930s, living in the small town of Milton in the Potteries:

Hollywood child star Shirley Temple. In the 1930s her curls and polka-dot dresses marked the beginning of the modern craze for child fashions as thousands of six- to eight-year-olds mimicked her looks

I saw these coupons in my mother's ladies' magazines for free samples of cold cream and powder and vanishing cream and such like. So I sent off for them and when they came I tried them out. I was only allowed out one evening a week and I had to be in by nine o'clock: I never dared to be late! Anyway, my father found out about the make-up and went wild. He called me a fast woman, though I didn't know what that was, and my mother threw all the make-up on the fire and said I had disgraced the whole family to the street. She never wore make-up and my father said, 'What's good enough for your mother's good enough for you.'

Younger girls, too, were being influenced by the glamour of Hollywood. Child stars, like Shirley Temple with her sweet, curly locks of hair and red and white polka dot dresses, were setting the fashion for thousands of six, seven and eight year olds. The cinema of the 1930s reinforced the trend by staging Shirley Temple look-alike competitions with prizes for the young winners. Some of these young girls were now not so keen to chase about in the fields and streets for fear of spoiling their looks.

Other 'modern' ideas – often, again, coming from America – were changing attitudes and behaviour. Progressive thinkers were arguing that the body was nothing to be ashamed of, and that sex and sex differences should be openly discussed and aired. The 'free' schools, like Summerhill and Beacon Hill, were casting aside the strict sex segregation of the past. Classes – even dormitories – were mixed, and boys and girls played together freely. Nudity was not frowned upon; indeed at Beacon Hill it was seen to be an integral part of self-expression through, in particular, modern dance. Harriet Ward was a pupil there in the mid 1930s:

We did that kind of 'free expression' dancing associated with people like Isadora Duncan. In summer dancing might take place on the lawn, barefoot and even in the nude if the weather was suitable. We were made to feel that there was nothing shameful about nudity, and we also had nude bathing in the summer. I don't remember classes in sex education as such, but the facts of procreation in animal, human and plant life were certainly taught in science lessons – natural science was a strong theme at Beacon Hill – and we had lots of animals, fish tanks with newts and tadpoles and so on, as most primary schools do today. The main point is that children's questions were always answered. I remember at one school council meeting when I was eight or nine, a special effort was made to explain what a 'bugger' was, to check a small outbreak of nudging and giggling which had been set off by some incident or other.

Leisure activities, too, were gradually becoming less sharply sex segregated. There were various rambling and hiking clubs which allowed boys and girls to go out together. But by far the most significant development was the founding of the Wood-craft Folk, an alternative youth organization intended specifically for children of the labour movement. Set up in 1925, the Woodcraft Folk was the first youth organization explicitly for both boys and girls. The emphasis was on co-education and equality and, as Henry Fair, one of the founding members, recalls it caused quite a stir at that time:

There was still the Victorian idea in 1925 that any girl that went about in shorts was already half-way to purgatory! And for boys and girls to camp together was terrible. I was running a camp down at Ashstead in the early days of the Folk and there was a scout troop in an adjacent field. And the scout leader came over because he was interested to see what he thought was a very well-planned camp. And he said, 'I see you've got girls here! Who walks around the tents at night-time to see that the boys don't go into the girls' tents?' I said, 'You have an awful mind haven't you?' I told him that the more you get a natural association of boys and girls the less likely it is that things are happening which he was obviously frightened of. It was difficult at the initial stages.

Nevertheless, the Woodcraft Folk flourished. By the 1930s, there were some 4000 members, and mixed camps and rambles were taking place up and down the country. It was, for its time, a breakthrough: it provided an environment in which boys and girls could muck about together without sexual connotations being attached to their behaviour. For the children themselves, it was all great fun, as Joyce Smith from the Tooting Folk in London, recalls:

Walking and climbing and camping – we had particularly wonderful camps – I suppose that's really why we joined to begin with. We camped out weekend after weekend and we used to hike every Sunday. There was not a Sunday, say from October round to March, when we didn't have a hike, including Boxing Day! And we'd get up to our necks in mud in the middle of winter, but the frosty air and the cold wind would tan our faces and immediately we went into the warm atmosphere of the underground, our faces would start to glow, and people would look at us and say 'Good God, where have you been?' It was a marvellous experience: the kids with their rucksacks on, green jerkins, absolutely tanned, laughing and singing, it was a joy to see.

But by far the greatest changes in attitudes towards children and their sexuality have come in the post-war years – and it

'Free expression' dancing at Beacon Hill School in the 1930s

was these changes that have led to the fears that the old innocence has gone. What has happened is that there has been a commercialization – and in turn sexualization – of the world of childhood.

By the 1950s, Britain had recovered from the austerity of the war years, and for most families these were, indeed, 'the never had it so good' years. Increasing prosperity meant that many families had far more money to spend on their children, and one upshot of this was the growth of a fashion industry for children. The arrival of man-made synthetic fabrics in the late 1940s, and of mass-produced ready-to-wear clothing, led to bright and exciting new designs. Ladybird were the first of the large companies to recognize the importance of the children's market, and as early as 1948 were marketing the first child's T-shirt. By the early 1960s Ladybird were spearheading a new marketing strategy designed to appeal not to parents but to young children themselves through carefully aimed tie-in Ladybird competitions, story books, and even an Adventure Club with its own comic. There was arising a generation of consumer-conscious children, critically concerned about how they looked.

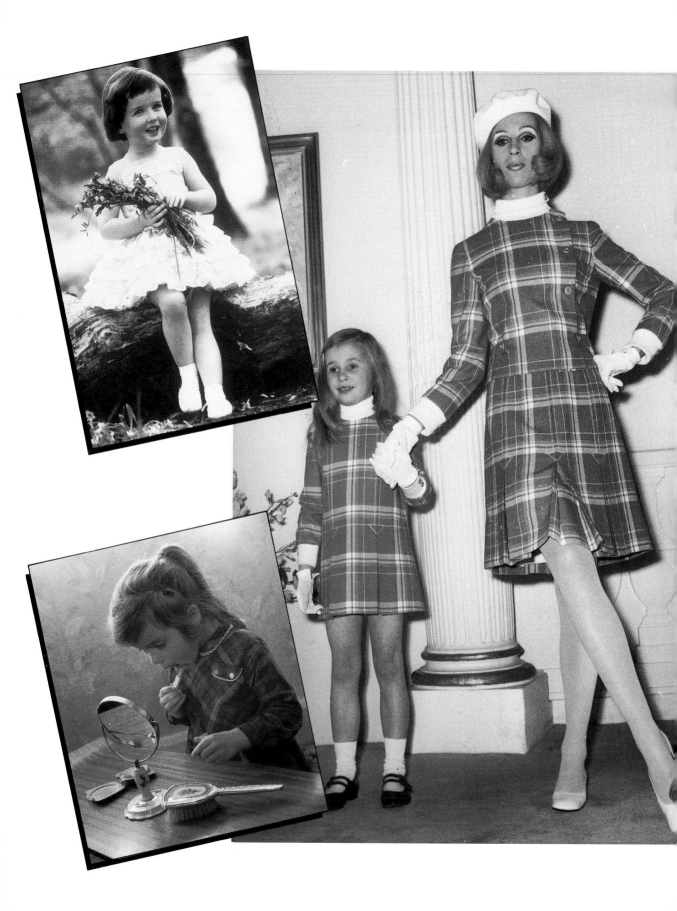

This increasing interest in the appearance of children was reflected in the growth of beauty competitions for young girls. The most famous of these was the 'Miss Pears' competition. In 1958 the Pears soap manufacturing company hit upon the bright idea of promoting their soap through appealing, pretty young girls' faces, chosen annually on the basis of a nationwide competition. In 1959, aged three years, Sue Fowler became the second Miss Pears:

It was actually my godfather, who was a keen amateur photographer, who persuaded my parents to send the photograph in. My parents are very private people and they were practically bludgeoned into it. When they announced it they said my father was in court at the time of the crowning, but they forgot to say he was a solicitor on the right side of the dock! It disrupted our lives quite a lot and I remember all the fuss of dressing up nicely and being crowned by Bernard Bresslaw and going to the celebration parties afterwards. I had lots of photos taken – they even took them of me when I was asleep!

But arguably the greatest force for change was television. During the 1950s the BBC had adopted an extremely paternalistic attitude towards children: their children's programmes had no hint of realism and certainly nothing to do with romance or sexuality. There was a close-down hour between six and seven so that parents could get their children to bed and this formed a rigid demarcation point between children's and adult's television. But by the early 1960s, this was beginning to change. Increasingly, older children stayed up late, watching adult programmes which by now had an air of social realism. And ITV started broadcasting, with regular slots for advertisements thus providing an opportunity for advertisers to target the new child market.

At the same time, the new youth culture – which had emerged during the 1950s as a result of the increase in leisure time and rising incomes of young adults – was filtering down to children. Again television, along with radio, played an important role in promoting this development. Watching their idols on programmes like 'Ready, Steady, Go', young children of eleven and twelve aspired to be part of this new culture. And, in turn, the new music and fashion industries increasingly saw children as important purchasers of their highly sexualized products.

Young teenagers would spend increasing amounts of time and money on their appearance. Girls, in particular, would spend hours preparing to go out on a Saturday night. The real devotees of fashion – most of them girls – no longer wanted to go off rambling and hiking or join in competitive games for fear that they might ruin their hairstyles or make-up or chip their carefully grown finger nails. Trish Hood was a 'Mod' growing up in Bristol in the 1960s:

I was always getting into trouble at school over make-up and clothes and nail varnish. They used to want the girls to look prim and proper and be very plain but I just couldn't stand it. I remember once I was caught wearing nail varnish and I was taken into the chemistry laboratory and the teacher poured acid over my nails to get it off. It really hurt! What I hated most of all, though, was going through the showers after our games lesson. I think the main reason was that it ruined my hair-do and wrecked my make-up. So I'd knock off; I'd just walk off home when it was games lessons to get out of it.

Such styles of behaviour and dress increasingly brought young schoolchildren into conflict with their teachers. The Maltby twins – Tony and Ray – were 'Mods', proudly

Below left: 'Mods', pictured here at a dance in the early 1960s, reflect the sexualization of childhood through their emphasis on adult fashion and make-up

Below right: Scunthorpe twins, Tony and Ray Maltby, in 1967, before school rules had forced them to trim their 'sideboards' by a sixteenth of an inch. This dispute led to a local school strike and their eventual expulsion

displaying their fine 'sideboards'. But the headmaster at their Scunthorpe school saw this as a breach of school rules which said that sideboards should not be more than halfway down the ears, and in October 1967 the fifteen-year-old twins were sent home and ordered to trim their hair. This eventually involved the Education Minister and led to a strike with over 100 fellow pupils staying away in sympathy. Tony Maltby:

We went into school when the whistle went and were sent into lessons. We were in the middle of Bible study when Mr Chapman, the headmaster, sent for us. He had two of the school governors with him and he measured our sideboards and said they were not acceptable and we would have to go home. I think we were sent home in all about a dozen times and all the lads in our class, 4C, walked out of school in support of us. They were disgusted at the way we'd been treated. Their parents had given them permission to walk out if we weren't admitted and there was a protest petition with 600 signatures. We had a meeting and arranged to give our friends a signal if we were being sent home again. Ray used his comb as we came out of the headmaster's room and this was the signal: they all walked out. I think they were caned for that. It was a joke by today's standards. But our father was worried sick about the whole affair and the ban broke his heart.

But it was probably girls – who were generally more fashion-conscious than boys – who came into conflict with the school authorities most often. Wearing mini-skirts and make-up was a regular source of contention, and often girls would have their transistor radios banned from school premises. At Borehamwood in Hertfordshire the police were even called in to stop the girls holding rock'n'roll parties in the street during their dinner breaks. Brenda Martin was one of these rock'n'rolling girls:

There were about thirty of us and we used to spend our dinnertime breaks rocking and rolling outside this record shop in Leeming Road. There was Tommy Steele and his *Singing the Blues*, but it was Elvis that really got us going: *Jailhouse Rock*, *You Ain't Nothing But a Hound-Dog* and *Heartbreak Hotel*. And there was Tab Hunter's *Young Love*. We spent all our money on chips and make-up. I remember we bought Miner's Rock'n'Roll pink lipstick for one and six: spent half our dinner money on it! The record shop used to put the records on and we'd dance. I suppose someone must have complained. The TV cameras arrived, and when they interviewed us we should have been back at school – we were all in hot water. I remember the disappointment when the school caretaker was interviewed and speaking with a very 'put on' posh accent and sided with our headmaster. We always thought he was on our side and we hated him after that! We hated them for taking away our lunchtime sessions and banning us from leaving school at lunchtime, and they banned us from wearing our lime-green fluorescent socks, but we put them on outside the school gates. I suppose we felt we were rebels: it's funny when you think about it now.

Increasingly, young teenagers spent more and more of their time, energy and money on this new youth culture. Pop groups like the Beatles and the Rolling Stones would be greeted wherever they went by crowds of screaming, hysterical schoolgirls. These girls were 'in love' with their idols – but it was, of course, love on a fantasy level.

But many were having their first sexual experience at a younger age. During the 1960s 'free love' came into vogue and, while it passed most teenagers by, more and more thirteen to sixteen year olds were experimenting with sex. One study in 1964 found that nearly one in three boys and one in four girls had had sexual intercourse before the age of sixteen. Ignorance about contraception meant that many unwanted pregnancies resulted and the problem of the schoolgirl mum hit the headlines. Sue Stapleton from Birmingham was fourteen years old when she discovered she was pregnant:

I suppose I was always a bit of a rebel. I went to a secondary modern in Birmingham, and in my spare time I liked to go to coffee bars and listen to rock'n'roll and all that. When I was fourteen I had a boyfriend who was eighteen – I suppose he was a bit of a teddy boy. We'd go on burn-ups on motor bikes over to Bromsgrove. We'd just hang around. I got pregnant the first time I ever made love. I was fourteen. It was awful. My mother was quite supportive but I was ostracized by everyone at school. They acted like they might catch it from me. My father went mad; he didn't want me in the house. So I had to go to a Salvation Army mum-and-baby home in Handsworth Wood. I was there for six months before the baby was born. I wanted to keep her but I had no money and no home of my own – how could I? So I had to arrange to have her adopted when she was three months old. When she grew up she managed to trace me and now we're really good friends.

In the 1970s and 1980s the pressure to be fashionable and 'sexual', if only in appearance, has reached down to younger children, not yet in their teenage years. In the 1970s, pop groups like the Bay City Rollers emerged, aiming directly at the teeny- and 'weeny'-bopper market (as these young pop enthusiasts came to be known). Discos for the under elevens were opened, drawing large and regular crowds. Even the Brownies have succumbed to the demands of today's young

Sue Stapleton, aged fourteen, with her baby Kim at a Salvation Army mother-and-baby home in Handsworth Wood in Birmingham in 1962. As more and more teenagers experimented with sex in the 1960s so the number of 'schoolgirl mothers' grew

children, starting their own discos. The fashion industries direct their advertising and products at younger and younger children, with make-up kits and designer fashions for five year olds. Indeed, children as young as two and three are now quite fashion conscious, ready to reject the hand-me-downs which a generation before knew so well. 'Poppet power' has arrived.

By the age of nine and ten, children have become remarkably sophisticated in their taste in clothes – and what they're demanding is 'adult' fashions. For the first time since before the First World War children's clothing designers are essentially simply scaling down adult fashions rather than creating specific children's lines. With adults themselves becoming far more casual in their dress, it is now quite often difficult to distinguish – at least at a glance – between children and their parents.

Initially it was girls who showed most interest in this fashion culture, wearing make-up before they reached their teens and dieting to look more feminine. But increasingly these trends have also affected boys who now spend nearly as much money on fashionable clothing as girls. It is a far cry from the days when they were happy to wear short trousers – now no longer seen – until their early teens. Young teenagers' lives are increasingly dominated by how they look and how they appear to the opposite sex. The avoidance of spots, for example, has become an obsession of these adolescent years.

These concerns are sharpened by the fact that many now have boyfriends and girlfriends at a younger and younger age. During the 1970s and 1980s, increasing numbers of children, aged ten, eleven or twelve, had girlfriends and boyfriends of the opposite sex.

These relationships between young boys and girls are invariably innocent, but they can nevertheless be very emotionally significant for the children involved. The problem pages of popular girls' magazines like *Jackie, Hi, Blue Jeans* and *Girl* graphically reveal the pressures of modern childhood. Large numbers of letters arrive each day from girls worried about acne, being overweight or losing their boyfriends. This letter was signed 'Depressed Girl Fan':

I would really like to have a boyfriend. Most of my friends have them and I feel left out. I have a few boyfriends who are just friends to me and nothing else. I am quite attractive and it isn't my looks that put boys off. I don't know what it is. Some nights when I go to bed I cry myself to sleep. I have felt like this for about a year now. Please help me.

Overleaf: Girls of the 1980s: Saturdays spent shopping with friends are a far cry from the harsh child labour of their grandparents

This trend towards having early boy and girlfriends has created new tensions between children and their parents. This is particularly true among some of the ethnic communities, where traditional values are still strong. Asian girls are often at odds with their fathers, who believe that after puberty they should not mix with boys. Many will change their clothes before they come home for fear of risking their father's wrath at the sexual provocativeness of western dress.

More generally, there is a fear among parents that the innocence, long associated with childhood, has been tainted by a knowledge of the secrets of the adult world. Children have access through television to a sexual world once the preserve of adults. The pop cultures of today, typified by groups such as the Pet Shop Boys, Wet Wet Wet and Bros, is more overtly erotic than ever before. And parents increasingly worry that videos have introduced young children of six, seven or eight to 'perverted' and 'deviant' sexual practices. As a result of all these trends, there is a widespread feeling that children are growing up too young – that childhood is disappearing.

But if we look across the experience of childhood as a whole it is clear these fears are exaggerated. Despite the pressures on children to become sexual at a younger age, there have been many gains in the post-war years in attitudes towards children's sexual development. There is, for example, a much more relaxed and open approach to the sex education of the young. The sexual myths and the sexual ignorance which haunted generations of children and young people are gradually being dispelled. Also, despite panics about children's interest in sex and the prevalence of child sex abuse, there is no doubt that children today are generally given far greater protection than was the case in the early years of the century. We have seen throughout this book a growing concern to protect children and to allow them to grow up and explore the world around them free from adult responsibilities. The days of child labour are, with a few, small exceptions, long gone. There is instead a much more child-centred world, where children can enjoy themselves, released from the pressure of work at home and in the factory. What we have seen in this chapter is a change in the nature and experience of childhood rather than its demise. Although children today are more worldly wise than they were earlier in the century, childhood as a distinct and protected stage of life is still very much alive and well. The twentieth century remains very much the century of the child.

Further Reading

Good all-round introductory books and surveys of the history of childhood are: Colin Ward, *The Child in the City* (The Architectural Press, 1977) and *The Child in the Country* (Robert Hale, 1988); James Walvin, *A Child's World*, (Penguin, 1982); John Burnett, *Destiny Obscure: Autobiographies of Childhood, Education and Family from the 1820s to the 1920s* (Penguin, 1984); Carol Adams, *Ordinary Lives: A Hundred Years Ago* (Virago, 1982); Thea Thompson, *Edwardian Childhoods* (Routledge and Kegan Paul, 1981); I. Pinchbeck and M. Hewitt, *Children in English Society, Volume Two* (Routledge and Kegan Paul, 1969) and Linda Pollock, *Forgotten Children* (Cambridge University Press, 1983); A. J. and D. K. Pierce, *Victorian and Edwardian Children from Old Photographs* (Batsford, 1980).

For Chapter One on child labour: John Springhall, *Coming of Age: Adolescence in Great Britain 1860–1960* (Gill and Macmillan, 1986); Standish Meacham, *A Life Apart: The English Working Class 1890–1914* (Thames and Hudson, 1977); Pamela Horn, *The Victorian Country Child* (Sutton, 1985) and *The Rise and Fall of the Victorian Servant* (Gill and Macmillan, 1975); Jennifer Tann, *Children at Work* (Batsford, 1981).

For Chapter Two on parental and family relationships and child welfare: Elizabeth Roberts, *A Woman's Place: An Oral History of Working-Class Women, 1890–1940* (Basil Blackwell, 1984); Paul Thompson, *The Edwardians* (Paladin, 1979); Jane Lewis, *The Politics of Motherhood: Child and Maternal Welfare in England 1900–1939* (Croom Helm, 1980); Christina Hardyment, *Dream Babies: Child Care from Locke to Spock* (Jonathan Cape, 1983); Diana Dick, *Yesterday's Babies: A History of Babycare* (Bodley Head, 1987); Sue Sharpe, *'Just Like a Girl': How Girls Learn to be Women* (Penguin, 1976).

For Chapter Three on play, children's games and youth movements: Iona Opie and Peter Opie, *The Lore and Language of Schoolchildren* (Oxford University Press, 1959), *Children's Games in Street and Playground* (Oxford University Press, 1969) and *The Singing Game* (Oxford University Press, 1985); Alasdair Roberts, *Out To Play: The Middle Years of Childhood* (Aberdeen University Press, 1980); Kenneth and Marguerite Fawdrey, *English Dolls and Toys* (Ernest Benn, 1979); Mary Cadogan and Patricia Craig, *You're a Brick, Angela! The Girls' Story, 1839–1985* (Gollancz, 1976); John Springhall, *Youth, Empire and Society: British Youth Movements 1883–1940* (Croom Helm, 1977); Michael Rosenthal, *The Character Factory: Baden-Powell and The Origins of the Boy Scout Movement* (Collins, 1986).

For Chapter Four on children's educational institutions, reformatories, industrial schools etc.: Steve Humphries, *Hooligans or Rebels: An Oral History of Working-Class Childhood and Youth 1889–1939* (Basil Blackwell, 1981); N. Middleton, *When Family Failed* (Gollancz, 1971); D. G. Pritchard, *Education and the Handicapped, 1760–1960* (Routledge and Kegan Paul, 1963); Jonathan Gathorne-Hardy, *The Public School Phenomenon* (Hodder and Stoughton, 1977) and *The Rise and Fall of the British Nanny* (Weidenfeld and Nicolson, 1985); W. A. C. Stewart, *Progressives and Radicals in English Education, 1750–1970* (Macmillan, 1972); Ian Gibson, *The English Vice* (Duckworth, 1978); Lionel Rose, *Young Offenders and the Law* (Batsford, 1984); Robert Roberts, *A Ragged Schooling* (Manchester University Press, 1976); Carol Dyhouse, *Girls Growing Up in Late Victorian and Early Edwardian England* (Routledge and Kegan Paul, 1981).

For Chapter Five on children's gangs, rivalries, friendships and outsiders, very little has been written but autobiographies, helped into print by community publishers, are a good source. There are also some excellent regional oral history archives of tape recorded interviews with older people: for details contact the Oral History Society, c/o Department of Sociology, University of Essex, Colchester, Essex CO4 3SQ; or the National Sound Archive, 29 Exhibition Road, London SW7 2AS. Of those books published the following are useful: Deborah Derrick, *Illegitimate: The Experience of People Born Outside Marriage* (National Council for One Parent Families, 1986); J. L. Watson, *Between Two Cultures* (Basil Blackwell, 1979).

For Chapter Six on changing sexual attitudes and the debate about the end of childhood: Steve Humphries, *A Secret World of Sex, Forbidden Fruit: The British Experience, 1900–1950* (Sidgwick and Jackson, 1988); Jeffrey Weeks, *Sex, Politics and Society* (Longman, 1981); Neil Postman, *The Disappearance of Childhood* (W. H. Allen, 1985); Ann Mitchell, *Children in the Middle: Living through Divorce* (Tavistock, 1985).

Picture Acknowledgements We would like to thank the following for permission to reproduce the photographs and illustrations in this book:
Barnardo Film Library: 18/19, 38, 55, 92/3, 120/1, 125; Beamish Open Air Museum: 12/13, 41; Len Bradbrook: 129; Bradford Heritage Recording Unit: 6/7, 21, 27, 100; Bradford Library: 44; Nora Clark: 15; Colindale Newspaper Library: 104/5; Documentary Photography Archive, Manchester: 14, 26, 48/9, 52 (top), 103, 126, 158/9; Ewan Duff: 84; Girl Guide Association; 153, 154/5; Greater London Council Picture Library: 94/5, 96, 106/7, 132/3; Richard and Sally Greenhill: 58/9, 114, 172/3; Highgate Institute: 50/1; Hodder and Stoughton: 156; Jack Hulme/Yorkshire Art Circus: 17; BBC Hulton Picture Library: 30/1, 52 (bottom), 57, 73 (top), 74/5, 80, 98, 99, 108/9 (bottom), 112/13, 137, 140, 148/9, 150, 151; Emma Jones: 131; Kobal Collection: 162; Peter Lawrence: 46; London Sound and Video Archive: i, 73 (bottom); Lord Bath 8/9; Billie Love Collection: 69, 70; Ethel McEvoy: 16; Maltby family: 169; Chris Makepeace: 18, 45; NSPCC: 42, 119; Oldham Local Interest Centre: 91; Photosource: 144/5, 168; Popperfoto: 22, 28, 33, 34/5, 36/7, 68, 77, 83, 86, 110, 111, 142/3, 166 (centre and bottom); RNIB: 108/9 (top); William Rushton: 146; Salford Library: 19; Salvation Army: 10/11, 20, 24/5, 116/17; Tim Smith: 85, 138/9; Sue Stapleton: 170; John Topham Picture Library: title, 60/1, 63, 64/5, 66, 72, 76, 79, 88/9; Harriet Ward: 165; Welbeck Public Relations Ltd: 166 (top).

Index